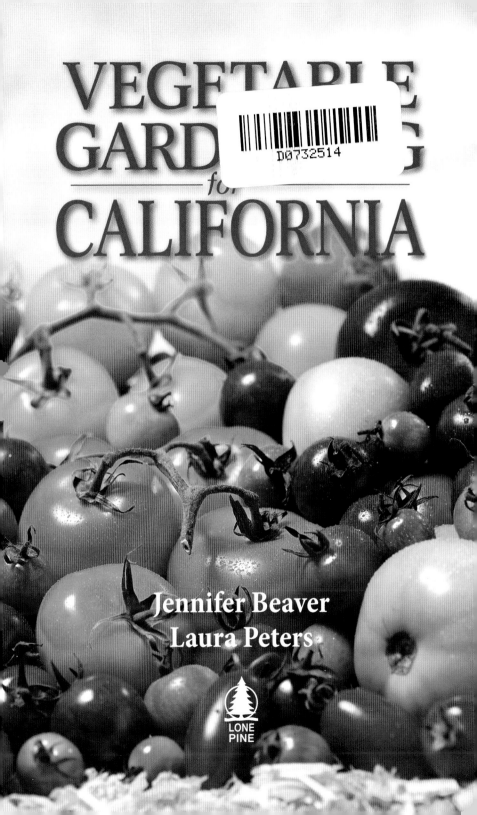

VEGETABLE
GARDENING
for
CALIFORNIA

Jennifer Beaver
Laura Peters

LONE
PINE

The Distributor: Lone Pine Publishing

1808 B Street, Suite 140
Auburn, WA USA 98001
Website: www.lonepinepublishing.com

Publisher's Cataloging-In-Publication Data
(Prepared by The Donohue Group, Inc.)

Beaver, Jennifer.
    Vegetable gardening for California / Jennifer Beaver and Laura Peters.

    p. : col. ill., maps ; cm.

    Includes index.

    ISBN: 978-976-650-053-5

    1. Vegetable gardening—California. 2. Plant selection—California. I. Peters, Laura, 1968–
II. Title.

SB321.5.C25 B42 2012

635/.09794

Photography: All photos are by Laura Peters except: All-America Selections 160a, 229b; Sandra Bit 6; Franky De Meyer 95a; Tamara Eder 18a, 46, 50, 55a, 181b, 185b, 249, 258a; Elliot Engley 31, 32a; Jen Fafard 42, 102, 123; Derek Fell 9, 24, 64a, 65a&b, 69b, 71, 98b, 114a, 115b, 133a, 145b, 165a&b, 173, 181a, 183a, 185a, 205b, 213, 214, 225a, 226b, 231a&b, 232a&b, 233, 234, 235, 236a&b, 237, 253a, 255; Saxon Holt 159a&b, 160b, 200a, 209b, 215; iStock 1, 113b, 199b, 230; Liz Klose 48, 75, 87a, 135a, 139b, 187a, 222b, 239b, 251, 252b; Trina Koscielnuk 116; Scott Leigh 109; Janet Loughrey 81a; Tim Matheson 25, 26, 27a&b, 29a, 30, 40, 44, 45a, 49, 52a, 55b, 56, 58; Marilyn McAra 164b; Kim O'Leary 53; photos.com 3, 60–61, 197; Robert Ritchie 52b, 57; Nanette Samol 4, 21, 33, 34, 41, 62, 63, 66, 70, 74, 76a, 78, 82, 83b, 86, 87b, 88, 89b, 90, 92, 93, 94, 96, 98a, 100a&b, 101, 103b, 104a, 105b, 108, 110, 111, 112, 113a, 114b, 115a, 118a, 120, 124, 126, 129, 130, 132, 134, 138, 140b, 143, 144, 145a, 146a, 147, 149a&b, 150a&b, 152, 155a, 156a, 158, 161, 162, 163a, 164a, 166a, 167, 168, 170, 174, 177b, 179a, 180, 182a&b, 184a&b, 186, 192, 198, 202, 203, 205a, 206, 208, 212, 216, 221, 225b, 227a, 228, 238, 240b, 241a, 242b, 245, 247, 248, 252a, 253b, 254a&b, 256a; Paul Swanson 39all, 64b, 72a&b, 76b, 97, 119, 122b, 131, 133b, 135b, 136a, 139a, 140a, 142, 175, 183b, 187b, 188b, 190a, 191a, 196a&b, 204a&b, 239a; Sandy Weatherall 13, 14, 18b, 20, 29b, 43, 77, 84, 95b, 99a&b, 104b, 106a&b, 107, 148, 163b, 166b, 171, 172a, 220, 222a, 241b, 243a; Don Williamson 54.

PC: 16

Contents

Introduction

There's never been a better time to plant vegetables.

With abundant sunshine and a temperate climate, California is a gardener's paradise. Our problem is not what *will* grow, but what *to* grow. Yet California does not offer one-size-fits-all gardening. Larger than many countries and with a wide range of temperatures and climate conditions, California is a checkerboard of microclimates. When you're pulling up the last of your tomatoes in the north, your cousin in San Diego is just putting in his fall garden. Gardeners on the coast may wrestle with fog; over in Palm Springs and other desert regions, they suffer from too much sun.

And that's why you need a guide like this one. Portable, packed with specific information, this book can be as valuable as your favorite hoe or cultivator. It's a garden tool you'll use again and again.

Look around. You'll see beans scampering up courtyard trellises, ruffled lettuce peeking from front-yard borders and tomatoes popping out of pots. All over the country, gardening interest and information is at an all-time high. As a result, new vegetable varieties crop up all the time, and beloved heirlooms become the favorite of new generations. Our choices are hardier, faster and better-tasting than ever, and plant specialists continue to offer new, compact varieties to address our desire for small-space gardening.

Why grow vegetables? The short answer is, of course, because we want

to eat them. But that's only part of it. There are many reasons. You'll save money on your grocery bill. You'll save the environment by consuming fewer resources to get food to your table. You'll help wildlife by reducing the need to expand cultivated land. You'll avoid commercial pesticides.

And you'll discover wonderful and sometimes historic food you could never buy in the store. For example, you can grow the same kinds of vegetables that pioneering plantsman President Thomas Jefferson cultivated at Monticello, his Virginia estate,

in the 18th century. They're still available. By taking control of your own little plot of dirt, you'll get the opportunity to seek out interesting varieties and specialty items so you can dazzle your friends with purple broccoli and Russian tomatoes.

Many vegetables are beautiful as well as tasty. Don't hesitate to put them in with some of your ornamentals; take advantage of stunning foliage. Colors range from gray-green and greens so dark they're almost black to shades of red, purple, yellow, blue and bronze. Richly patterned and veined

Vegetables, like this lettuce, don't have to be grown in rows.

foliage sometimes contrasts with the leaf color. Foliage can be immense or delicate and feathery. Your beautiful landscape, full of unique and attractive edibles, will be the envy of the neighborhood.

Growing vegetables is easier than you think. Many would-be gardeners get discouraged before they begin. They envision the hard, sweaty labor involved in digging large, neat squares and rectangles; removing heavy rocks from the soil; and painstakingly laying out row after row of tiny seeds.

Fast forward to the home garden of the 21st century. While you can certainly do it the backbreaking traditional way, your friends are using no-dig raised beds and containers. They're putting them in back yards, front yards, side yards and balconies, on roofs and driveways and in hanging planters.

How much is enough? That's an individual choice, but it's easy to supplement what you buy by growing a few of your favorites. Two broccoli lovers, for example, will need only three to six plants. Do you like zucchini? Four zucchini plants—in shapes from round to long and cylindrical—will give you plenty to share with the neighbors.

As with any gardening, growing vegetables should be fun. They add unique colors and textures to your garden and your dinner plate. Experiment with a few new ones each year, and you may find yourself looking for space to add even more.

Vegetables with Interesting Foliage

Artichokes	Kale
Asparagus	Leeks
Cabbage	Lettuce
Carrots	Mustard
Chard	Rhubarb
Fennel	Squash

Zucchini plants can be very prolific.

California Gardening Regions

With more than 160,000 square miles, 58 counties, mountains, deserts, valleys, lakes and coastline, California has a diverse collection of growing conditions. Gardeners experience almost every imaginable situation somewhere in the state. Recorded temperatures range from -45° to 134° F. One region receives 161 inches of rain every year; another gets virtually none. Welcome to California!

Yet in spite of, or because of, the geographical diversity, California is an ideal place to grow a huge variety of vegetables. Some plants grow equally well in all parts of the state, and others will do better in one region over another. Understanding your geographical region will help you determine what to plant, and when. Keep in mind, however, that conditions can deviate greatly from garden to garden within a region. Broad factors include climate, season length and day length. Yet individual conditions such as soil type, microclimates, light and heat vary not only from garden to garden but also within a single garden. Supplement general guidelines with local knowledge. Talk to your neighbors and walk around the block. Visit the local garden center and ask lots of questions. Call your local county extension office. Join a local garden club.

Northern California has several distinct geographic areas—coast, inland valleys, mountains and desert. The northern California coast is the wettest area of the state, with cool days and nights and moderate, even temperatures. Frost is infrequent. Fog influences temperatures and growing conditions during the mostly dry summers from March to November.

Moving inland toward the valley, the fog lifts and temperature becomes more variable. Summers are hotter; winters are colder. The Sierra Nevada mountains block the heavy rains. Across the north, temperatures vary amazingly with a few miles. On a midsummer July day in coastal Half Moon Bay, the temperature could be a pleasant 64° F; travel 25 miles inland to Walnut Creek, and the temperature rises 20 degrees; by the time you go another 25 miles east and stop at Tracy, the temperature

California is an ideal place to grow a huge variety of vegetables.

is up to 95° F. The lesson: know your local weather.

The short, cool summers in parts of northern California present a few challenges. Many "summer" crops (tomatoes, peppers, eggplants) need a long period of warm weather to thrive. By researching short-season varieties, making use of season extenders such as cold frames and cloches, and knowing the micro-climates that exist in their own gardens, many gardeners in the northern area succeed with the most finicky warm-season crops.

Some of this region is prime gardening real estate. Between the Sierra Nevada and the coastal mountain ranges lies the 400-mile Central Valley, an incredibly fertile area that produces more than 350 different crops consumed by the entire country. Home gardeners here enjoy a nine-month growing period ideal for long-season crops.

Southern California also has coastal, mountain, valley and desert conditions. Famous world-wide for its ideal climate, gardeners here plant and harvest nearly year-round, often taking advantage of a second growing season in fall. In many areas, there is no frost from November to January. While northern California sometimes gets too much rain, southern California often suffers from too little.

Along the coast, temperatures remain moderate with little fluctuation. Coastal fog keeps things cool but makes it difficult to grow sun-lovers such as tomatoes and egg-plants. Slightly inland, gardeners have a harmonious climate with long, relatively cool, sunny days.

Farther inland, parts of the inland valley stay clear and hot without the marine influence. Temperatures can easily reach 100° F. High heat makes it difficult to grow cool-season crops such as spinach and lettuce. Again, these intrepid gardeners work with the climate by making smart choices for their individual plots of ground.

Peppers can be a challenge in northern California but will do well farther south.

To the east lies the desert, land of limited rainfall and extreme temperatures. Although known for its heat, the desert also gets periods of cold and occasional winter storms.

So how can you make sense of all this for your garden? Get to know these three pieces of climate information: hardiness zone, the last frost date of spring and the first frost date of fall. The hardiness zone (see map, below) is actually a temperature range; plants are rated based on the last zone that offers a decent chance of survival. If you picked up a plant labeled "hardy to Zone 9," for example, you would know that it would do fine in temperatures from 20° to 30° F, the coldest rating for that zone. If you

want to plant it in colder Zone 8, with a low 10° to 20° F rating, you would be taking a risk and might need to give the plant some extra care by placing it near a sunny wall or otherwise sheltering it from cold.

The frost dates provide a good estimate of season length (see maps, right). If you can depend on only a few frost-free months, choose plants that will survive a light frost or that will mature during your anticipated growing season. Such plants might be labeled "short season" or "early"; those that require a longer growing season are "long season" or "late." In California, the growing season ranges from only

Plant hardiness zones for California

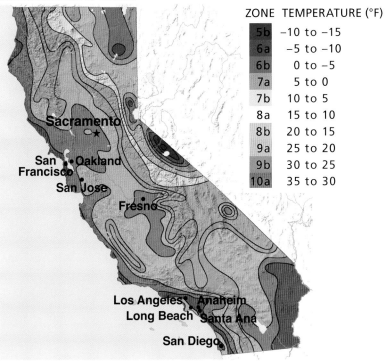

ZONE	TEMPERATURE (°F)
5b	−10 to −15
6a	−5 to −10
6b	0 to −5
7a	5 to 0
7b	10 to 5
8a	15 to 10
8b	20 to 15
9a	25 to 20
9b	30 to 25
10a	35 to 30

Spring and fall frost dates for California

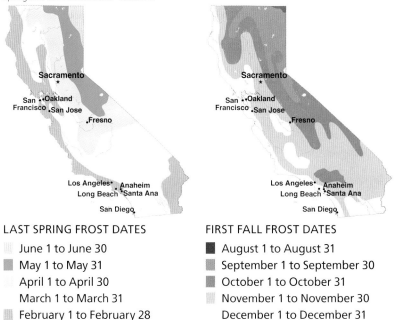

LAST SPRING FROST DATES

- June 1 to June 30
- May 1 to May 31
- April 1 to April 30
- March 1 to March 31
- February 1 to February 28

FIRST FALL FROST DATES

- August 1 to August 31
- September 1 to September 30
- October 1 to October 31
- November 1 to November 30
- December 1 to December 31

50 days high in the Sierras to a whopping 365 days in parts of southern California. Temperate areas in the Central Valley and along the coast may get from 225 to 300 days without frost, which essentially ends a growing season.

This information provides a good starting point but should not completely rule your planting decisions. Be flexible. An early, warm spring offers an excellent opportunity to set out a few plants. If spring is cold and wet, however, wait a week or two later than usual.

Special Considerations for California Gardeners

Throughout much of California, fall is a wonderful time to plant vegetables. The air and earth are still warm, and winter rains provide the only natural irrigation some areas receive all year. While long-season heat lovers like tomatoes and eggplants should wait until spring, cool-season vegetables like broccoli, spinach and lettuce are ready to go. Keep this in mind when consulting non-California gardening sources. Many are geared for traditional spring planting and may not mention our wonderful fall planting season.

Another climate-related issue is the chill factor. Some vegetables do better if exposed to chill, and possibly frost. Rhubarb, for example, thrives in the north; heat-loving artichokes favor the south. Chill requirements can vary greatly from vegetable to vegetable; check with a nursery specialist to find varieties that will do well in your garden.

Choosing Your Style

Vegetable gardens come in many forms and include a wide variety of plants. The neat rows of a traditional vegetable garden were adopted from the farm garden, and the attention paid to plant and row spacing is designed to make large numbers of plants more easily accessible. If you have plenty of space and want loads of vegetables, this style can work for you.

Today, many of us garden on smaller lots and often need to wedge a tomato or other vegetable into what we already have. Fortunately, it's not difficult. There are an unlimited number of ways to integrate vegetables into ground-level planting areas, raised beds and containers.

There is no need to segregate vegetables from ornamental plants. The French *potager*, or kitchen garden, mixes the two and is both decorative and functional. It generally consists of a symmetrical arrangement of raised beds. Plants are often repeated in a location in each bed rather than having one bed of all the same plant. Vegetables are combined with herbs and fruiting shrubs as well as edible flowers. Co-mingling plants is not only beautiful but also healthy. Variety reduces pests and diseases because it limits the number of susceptible plants in close proximity.

Another option is a square-foot garden. Dividing an area into square-foot increments provides a higher yield and neater garden. A 4-foot by 4-foot bed, for example, creates 16 smaller squares. In each square,

A traditional row (above)

Block planting (below)

plant as much as the single space will allow. Space-hogs such as tomato and squash get one square apiece; smaller vegetables such as radishes grow 16 to a square. After harvesting, plant something new.

As your garden grows and develops and you need to add new plants, think about adding edible ones. If you are replacing an existing perennial or shrub, perhaps you could replace it with asparagus or rhubarb—sturdy, hardy perennial choices. The wealth of annual options is nearly limitless.

Raised Bed Gardening

Raised beds are an ideal way to grow vegetables. Gardening in raised beds

When planting intensively, keep plants fairly close together but leave enough room for each one to grow. Many vegetables go from small seedlings to large mature plants very quickly. Give them some room to spread and increase your yield.

means less work. Beds can be raised up to whatever height suits you. When you raise the level of the garden, there's little need to bend over or squat, and with the addition of a shallow ledge on all sides, a gentle bend is all it takes to weed or harvest a 2-foot-high vegetable bed. In fact, the need for weeding will be drastically reduced.

A raised bed

A raised bed is simply a bottomless box placed on the ground, which could be your lawn or your concrete driveway. As long as the drainage is good, it will work. One you've filled the box with good soil mix and compost (but not garden soil!), you're ready to go.

There are many advantages to this method. You can place your garden where you want without digging; the soil in it is loose, fresh and easily worked; and because your raised bed warms up earlier than the surrounding earth, you can plant your vegetables earlier.

Vegetable Gardening with Limited Space

There are many options for gardeners with limited gardening space. With populations growing and city densities increasing, more and more people are learning about the possibilities of their small spaces and discovering just how productive they can be. You don't

Tomatoes do very well in containers.

Use containers to turn your balcony into a garden (above).

need a large backyard to grow vegetables—you just need to get creative. Vegetables can grow in just about any space, whether in the ground or in some form of container.

California gardeners have embraced container gardening because of its ease and versatility. Many vegetables grow cheerfully on a balcony, deck, porch or patio. Containers can be placed anywhere and take up little space, can be moved around and sometimes offer more control than gardening directly in the ground.

Even a small container can be used to grow vegetables (below).

Just about anything can be used as a container, as long as there is adequate drainage and enough space for the vegetable plant that will be spending its life there. Use good-quality potting soil for containers, and add compost to the mix as a natural source of nutrients. Do not use soil from the garden, as it can compact, making it tough for roots to thrive.

Do you live in an apartment? Your balcony or front porch is a great place for a container vegetable garden. Think quality rather than quantity and enjoy every pea, tomato and herb you pick.

Condominium owners may even be able to garden on the roof. Run the idea by your condo board. People often jump on board immediately when they find out that they can grow food mere steps away from their front door, and they'll help to set it

Vertical gardening expands your garden space upward (above).

Community gardens are a great option for city dwellers with limited space (below).

up and maintain the plants so that they can reap the rewards at harvest.

If the only open space you have is vertical, then vertical gardening is the solution. Smaller, trailing and leafy plants can all be grown in containers that hang or attach to a wall or other vertical surface, such as a fence. Trellises, pyramids, obelisks and other vertical supports are great for vegetables that can grow upward rather than outward, rendering your precious space more efficient and resulting in higher yields and easier harvesting. For example, beans, peas and cucumbers can use supports such as netting, trellises and chain-link fences. Even hanging baskets are ideal for vertical spaces; try them for small, cascading cherry tomatoes.

Community gardens are another option for those who just do not have the space but really want to grow some of their own food. Community gardens are everywhere, from the smallest towns to the largest cities, and have so much more to offer than just a plot. It's an inexpensive, fun way to garden and to meet others who share your desire to be more self-sufficient. If you have too much at harvest time, donate it to your family, neighbors or the food bank. It doesn't take long to grow more than you can eat, and there is always someone who will appreciate the donation of delicious, nutritious, locally grown produce.

Organic Gardening

Organic gardening is defined as a method of raising plants without the usage of synthetic pesticides or

Try growing your vegetables organically.

fertilizers. Throughout the world, a bewildering array of bodies and institutions monitor and regulate what it means to be organic for commercial growers. Things are somewhat simpler for the home gardener.

Organic gardening starts with the choice to use natural methods to control weeds, diseases and pests. Doing so encourages beneficial insect populations and helps the environment. It boosts soil by maximizing

biological soil activity. Synthetic pesticides and fertilizers provide a quick fix that unfortunately may cause lasting harm. Some pesticides have been implicated in cancer and infertility and remain in the soil for generations. Synthetic fertilizers are often compared to drugs; those who use them may say their "vegetables are on crack." And like cocaine, it gives the plants a quick high and then depletes their energy.

Why grow organically? Studies have shown that organic vegetables are higher in nutrients. Certainly, it's better for the environment and future generations. Growing organically is not a quick fix, but an ongoing practice that puts you in touch with the rhythm of nature.

Produce is healthier when grown organically, without the use of synthetic chemicals (above).

Organic gardening is healthy for you and for the environment (below).

Getting Started

Finding the right mix of vegetables for your garden requires experimentation, creativity and persistence. Before you start planting, consider the growing conditions in your garden; your plant selection will be influenced by levels of light, soil type, amount of exposure and the plants' frost tolerance. Plants will be healthier and have fewer problems if grown in optimum conditions, so if your garden has hot, dry areas or low-lying damp places, select plants that prefer those conditions.

Make a sketch to help you visualize how various conditions can affect your planting decisions. Note shaded areas, low-lying or wet areas, exposed or windy sections, etc. Understanding your garden's growing conditions will help you learn where plants perform best and prevent costly and frustrating planning mistakes. Remember that these conditions change from season to season. Leafed-out trees cast shade where there once was sun, for example.

Light

There are four basic levels of light in a garden: full sun, partial shade (partial sun), light shade and full shade. Buildings, trees, fences and the position of the sun at different times of the day and year affect available light. Knowing what

Before you plant cabbage, make sure you have the ideal spot in your garden for it.

light is available in your garden will help you determine where to place each plant.

Plants in full sun locations, such as along south-facing walls, receive more than six hours of direct sunlight in single day. Locations classified as partial shade, such as east- or west-facing walls, receive direct sunlight for part of the day (four to six hours) and shade for the rest. Light shade locations receive shade for most or all of the day, though some sunlight does filter through to ground level. An example of a light shade location might be the ground under a small-leaved tree such as a birch. Full shade locations, which can include the north side of a house, receive no direct sunlight.

For greater accuracy, pick up an inexpensive light meter that calculates the amount of sun in a particular location. Move it around until you find the right place to grow vegetables—usually in full sun.

Most vegetables thrive in full sun.

Soil

Soil quality is an extremely important element of a healthy garden. You'll often hear people say, "Feed the soil, not the plant." Roots rely on the air, water and nutrients held within the soil. Of course, plants also depend on soil to hold them upright. In return, plants benefit soil by breaking down large clumps, binding small particles to prevent erosion and reducing the amount of exposed surface. When plants die and break down, they add organic nutrients to soil and feed beneficial microorganisms.

Soil is made of different-sized particles. Sand is the largest; water drains quickly from sandy soil, and nutrients tend to get washed away. Sandy soil does not compact easily because the large particles leave air pockets between them. Clay particles, the smallest, can be seen only through a microscope. Clay holds the most nutrients, but it also compacts easily and has little air space. Clay is slow to absorb water and equally slow to let it drain. Silt is midway between sand and clay in particle size. Most soils are a combination of sand, clay and silt and are called loams.

Healthy soils smell sweet and nutty and contain a wide variety of particle sizes, shapes and weights. Most importantly, healthy soils are teeming with life—fat earthworms, tiny microarthropods, such as spiders and mites, and organisms seen only with a microscope, including one-celled protozoa, fungal mycelia and myriads of bacteria. In healthy soils, the cycle of life is constantly turning, recycling dead matter into fuel for living organisms. Precious minerals are continuously returned to the topsoil, and nutrients are released by all the organisms that reside in the soil.

However, most soils, perhaps even those in your own backyard, are completely devoid of life. Depleted of organic matter, they merely serve to hold struggling plants upright. Often the result of erosion, time and chemicals, such depleted soil is not the best home for your vegetables.

Organic amendments will improve any soil.

Plants grown here are compromised and vulnerable and make perfect targets for disease and insects. Fortunately, adding organic matter such as compost can turn them back into balanced, living communities.

Soil's pH level (the scale on which acidity or alkalinity is measured) also influences the availability of nutrients. Most plants thrive in soil with a pH between 5.5 and 7.5. For plants that prefer a pH that varies greatly from that of your garden soil, use planters or create raised beds so you can easily control and alter the pH level. Reduce soil acidity by adding horticultural lime or wood ashes; increase it with sulfur, peat moss or pine needles.

Potatoes prefer an acidic soil.

Consider buying testing kits from a garden center or sending a soil sample to a soil-testing lab. In addition to analyzing the pH and nutrients, some soil tests will also reveal the presence of industrial or chemical pollutants. These are of particular concern when growing vegetables because plants may absorb them—not a good thing, because we consume them! Gardens near freeways and industrial areas are particularly at risk. There is a relatively simple solution, however. If your garden soil is too toxic for vegetables, get some potting soil and grow your veggies in raised beds or containers.

Soil type and terrain also affect drainage. Plants that prefer well-drained soil and do not require a large amount of moisture grow well on a hillside garden with rocky soil. Improve water retention in these areas by adding organic matter. Water-loving plants are ideal for low-lying areas that retain water for longer periods. Improve drainage by adding gravel, creating raised beds or using French drains or drainage tile.

Exposure

Your garden is exposed to wind, heat, cold and rain. Some plants are better adapted than others to withstand the potential damage of these forces. Buildings, walls, fences, hills, hedges, trees and even tall perennials influence and often reduce exposure.

Wind and heat are the elements most likely to cause damage. Both can rob plants of much-needed moisture. In areas of low rainfall, it's particularly important to monitor your plants. The sun can be very intense, and heat rises quickly on a sunny afternoon. Choose vegetables that tolerate or even thrive in hot weather for your garden's hot spots.

Too much rain can damage plants, as can over-watering. Mulch early in the season to prevent seeds or seedlings from being washed away in heavy rain. Most established plants beaten down by heavy rain will recover, but some are slower to do so. Waterlogged soil encourages root rot. Most edible plants prefer well-drained soil.

Hanging baskets are particularly susceptible to wind and heat exposure, losing water from the soil surface and the leaves. Hanging baskets look wonderful, but watch for wilting, and water the baskets regularly to keep them looking great.

A fence will often reduce exposure (above).

Radishes are hardy enough to withstand a light frost (below).

Frost Tolerance

When planting vegetables, consider their ability to tolerate an unexpected frost. The map on page 11 gives a general idea of when you can expect your last frost date. Your local garden center should be able to provide more precise information. Although frost is an infrequent issue in the south, it can devastate tropicals and other frost-tender plants.

Plants are grouped into three categories based on how tolerant they are of cold weather: hardy, half-hardy or tender.

Hardy plants tolerate low temperatures and even frost. They can be planted in the garden early and may survive long into fall or even winter.

They often fade in summer heat after producing an early crop. Many hardy vegetables are sown directly in the garden in the weeks before the last frost date and can be sown again in summer for a second crop in fall.

Half-hardy plants can tolerate a light frost but will be killed by a heavy one. These edibles can be planted out around the last frost date and will generally benefit from being started indoors from seed if they are slow to mature.

Tender plants have no frost tolerance and might suffer if the temperature drops to even a few degrees above freezing. These are often started early indoors and are not planted in the garden until the last frost date has passed and the ground has had a chance to warm up. These vegetables often tolerate hot summer temperatures.

Protecting plants from frost is relatively simple. Cover plants overnight with sheets, towels, burlap or even cardboard boxes—don't use plastic because it doesn't provide any insulation.

Eggplants are tender annuals that will do best in the warmest spot in your garden.

Preparing the Garden

You'll save time and effort later in the season and get better food if you take time to properly prepare your growing area. Get edibles off to a good start by minimizing weeds and adding organic material. For container gardens and raised beds, use potting soil. When used in containers, regular garden soil loses its structure and quickly compacts into a solid, poorly draining mass.

Tackle a garden bed by loosening soil with a large garden fork and removing weeds. Avoid working very wet or very dry soil; this breaks down air and water pockets and damages the soil, making it less fertile. Add good-quality compost and work it in using a spade, fork or rototiller. How much compost do you need? Plan on covering your garden with a 2- to 4-inch layer.

Or do it the easy way and create a no-dig lasagna garden. The name refers to the layering found in the Italian pasta dish. It's fast, organic and easy on the back. First, stake out your garden area. Cover it with cardboard or pads of newspaper to smother the grass. Soak it with water. Next, start your layers; 2 to 3 inches of coir or peat moss followed by 2 to 3 inches of organic material such as mulch, compost or grass clippings. Repeat until the pile reaches 18 to 24 inches. Soak your new gardening bed, and top with mulch. You can plant immediately or let it simmer for a while to decompose.

Organic matter is a small but important component of soil. It increases the water- and nutrient-holding capacity of sandy soil and binds together the large particles. In a clay soil, organic matter will increase the water-absorbing and draining potential by opening up spaces between the tiny particles. It will also add the most important element for an organic vegetable garden: micronutrients and microorganisms. Without these, your plants will become reliant on synthetic fertilizers rather than the beneficial components naturally found in healthy soil. Common organic additives for your soil include grass clippings, shredded leaves, peat moss, chopped straw and well-rotted manure.

The best evidence of a healthy soil is one filled with fat earthworms. Beyond earthworms is a vast array of life including insects, mites, spiders and various microorganisms, all of which aid plant life by helping to decay organic material and adding structure to the soil. Soil microorganisms live in the rhizosphere, directly adjacent to plant roots. This zone of soil contains elements such as sloughed root cells that provide nutrients for bacteria, fungi and nematodes.

These organisms are present in most soils, and enrichment will benefit your plants even more. You can amend your soil with such things as compost, worm castings and manure; regular amendments are best. Commercial mixtures containing naturally occurring biological agents are slowly becoming available.

Compost

Compost is what happens when organic matter—anything from leaves to rinds to coffee grounds—is broken down into a dense, nutrient-packed blend. An important element for vegetable gardening success, compost provides a double bonus because it adds nutrients and improves the soil structure. Any organic matter will work more efficiently if it has been composted first.

Lots of earthworms indicate healthy soil.

In natural environments, compost is created when leaves, plant bits and other debris are broken down on the soil surface. This process will also take place in your garden beds if you work fresh organic matter into the soil. However, the microorganisms that break down organic matter use the same nutrients as your plants. The tougher the organic matter, the more nutrients needed to break it down, thus robbing your plants of vital nutrients, particularly nitrogen. Also, fresh organic matter and garden debris might encourage or introduce pests and diseases to your garden.

Making your own compost is simple, convenient and uses up a lot of household waste that would otherwise wind up in a landfill. Start with a purchased or homemade pile or bin. This creates a controlled environment where organic matter can be fully broken down before being introduced to your garden. Organic material includes such things as leaves, grass, vegetable kitchen scraps and coffee grounds. Good composting methods also reduce the possibility of spreading pests and diseases. Many towns offer composting workshops and discounts on composters.

Creating compost is easy. You can speed up the process by following a few simple guidelines:

- Put in both dry and fresh materials. Use mostly dry matter, such as chopped straw, shredded leaves or sawdust. Fresh green matter, such as vegetable scraps, grass clippings or pulled weeds, breaks down quickly and produces nitrogen, which feeds the decomposer organisms while they break down the tougher dry matter.

- Alternately layer the green and dry matter and mix in small amounts of garden soil or

An assortment of compost bins

finished compost to introduce beneficial microorganisms. If the pile seems very dry, sprinkle on some water—the compost should be moist but not soaking wet, like a wrung-out sponge.

- Aerating speeds decomposition, so turn the pile or poke holes in it every week or two. A well-aerated compost pile can generate a lot of heat. Temperatures can reach 160° F or more. Such high temperatures destroy weed seeds and kill many damaging organisms. Most beneficial organisms are not killed until the temperature rises higher than 160° F. Some gardeners monitor the temperature near the middle of the pile with a thermometer attached to a long probe, similar to a large meat thermometer. Turning compost when the temperature reaches 160° F stimulates the heat process but prevents the temperature from becoming high enough to kill beneficial organisms.

- Don't put diseased or pest-ridden materials into your compost pile. If the damaging organisms are not destroyed, they could spread throughout your garden.

When you can no longer recognize what you put into the compost bin, and the temperature no longer rises upon turning, your compost is ready to be mixed into your garden beds. Getting to this point can take as little as one month.

If you don't have the time or space to create your own, buy bagged compost at a garden center.

Suitable materials for compost (above)

A compost thermometer (below)

Selecting Vegetable Plants

Many gardeners consider the trip to their local garden center an important rite of spring. Big-box retailers and garden centers increasingly stock new and heirloom vegetables along with old standbys. Other gardeners find it rewarding to start their own plants from seed. They take great delight in hunting down unusual varieties online and swapping seeds with like-minded friends.

Both methods have benefits, so you might want to use a combination of the two. Purchasing plants provides you with plants that are well grown, which is useful if you don't have the room or the facilities to start seeds. Transplants are more expensive but much less labor intensive than seeds, and more immediate. Growing vegetables from seed will require more time, space and effort—some seeds require specific conditions that are difficult to achieve in a house, or they have erratic germination rates, which makes starting them yourself impractical—but starting from seed offers you a far greater selection of species and varieties because seed catalogs often list many more plants than are offered at garden centers. It's fun and rewarding to know that you grew your food from scratch, but if growing plants from seed is new to you, then you might want to start with only a few seeds, just in case first attempts prove fruitless, so to speak. Starting from seed is discussed beginning on page 31.

When browsing for plants and seeds, you'll find references to the terms "hybrid" and "heirloom." Hybrids are generally newer selections bred for specific traits such as flavor, size, disease resistance or improved storability. Often developed for market growers

Garden centers have the knowledge and facilities to give plants a good start.

and food exporters, hybrids usually have traits that make them suitable for packing and transporting long distances without spoiling. Hybrids rarely come true to type from collected seed.

Heirloom refers to plant selections cultivated for generations. Many gardeners like the connection with history, knowing that their grandparents grew the same type of plant. Some of the most intriguing vegetable selections are heirlooms, and advocates say they are the tastiest. Heirloom seeds collected from the plants produce true-to-type offspring.

Purchased plants grow in a variety of containers. Some are sold in individual pots, some in divided cell-packs and others in undivided trays. Each type has advantages and disadvantages.

Plants in individual pots are usually well established and generally have plenty of space for root growth.

Most likely seeded in flat trays, then transplanted into individual pots, they are expensive due to the cost of labor, pots and soil.

Plants grown in cell-packs are less expensive and hold several plants, making them easy to transport. Since each plant is individual, it's easy to transplant. But because each cell is quite small, it doesn't take long for a plant to become root-bound.

The rootball of a root-bound plant (above)

Many gardeners purchase tomato seedlings rather than starting this versatile fruit from seed (below).

Plants grown in undivided trays have plenty of room for root growth and can be left in the trays longer than in other types of containers. Their roots tend to tangle, however, making the plants difficult to separate.

Regardless of the container, check the roots. If they're emerging from the container bottom or wrapped around the inside of the container in a thick web, they've been there too long. Such plants are slow to establish once transplanted.

What should you watch for when shopping? Look for compact plants with good color. Healthy leaves are firm and vibrant; unhealthy leaves may be wilted, chewed or discolored. Tall, leggy plants have usually been deprived of light. Check for any sign of insects and disease. Avoid sickly plants, even if they're a great deal. At best, they won't perform as well as the healthy ones. At worst, they may spread pests or diseases.

Before you leave the store, make sure you know what type of conditions your new plants prefer. Do they like sun? How much water do they need? You may find this information on the plant tag, but if not, question the staff.

When you bring plants home, water them if they are dry. Plants in small containers may require water more than once a day. Begin to harden them off so they can be transplanted into the garden as soon as possible. Hardening off is the process that allows your sheltered, greenhouse-grown plants to become accustomed to the outdoors. Place them in a lightly shaded spot each day and bring them in to a sheltered porch, garage or house each night for about a week to acclimatize them to your garden.

An unhealthy plant next to a healthy plant

Starting Vegetables from Seed

Dozens of catalogs offer edible plants to start from seed. Many gardeners spend their chilly winter evenings poring through seed catalogs and planning their spring, summer and fall gardens. Also check out the internet, local garden centers and seed exchange groups.

Starting from seed saves money, particularly if you want a lot of plants. The basic equipment is not expensive, and a sunny window provides a good launching area. Keep in mind that you may run out of room quickly if you enthusiastically plant more than two plant trays. Many gardeners start a few specialty plants themselves and then purchase the rest from a garden center.

Each plant in this book is accompanied by specific seed-starting information, if any is required. Following are some general guidelines for starting all seeds.

There are several options when selecting seed-starting containers. Cell-packs in trays with plastic dome covers are particularly easy. The cell-packs keep roots separated, and the tray and dome keep moisture in.

Other choices include regular ceramic or plastic pots, peat pots or peat pellets. The advantage to starting in peat pots or pellets is that you will not disturb the roots when transplanting because you plant the entire biodegradable container.

Use a growing mix (soil mix) intended for seedlings. Made from peat moss, vermiculite and perlite, these sterilized mixes have advanced water-handling capabilities that help them stay moist while draining appropriately.

Among other advantages, soil mixes prevent damping off, an issue caused by soil-borne fungi. The affected seedling looks like it has been pinched at soil level. The pinched area blackens, and the seedling topples over and dies. Using sterile soil mix, keeping soil evenly moist and maintaining good air circulation will prevent plants from damping off.

Fill pots or seed trays with soil mix and firm slightly. Soil that is too firmly packed will not drain well. Before planting, wet the soil to prevent seeds from getting washed around. Plant large seeds one or two to a cell.

Seed starting supplies

Vegetables to Start Indoors

This list is for those with a short growing season; southern California gardeners and others with longer temperate weather can direct sow these plants.

Artichokes	Eggplant
Broccoli and	Leeks
other *Brassica*	Okra
spp.	Peppers
Celery	Squash
Cucumbers	Tomatoes

Pot up well-developed seedlings until they can be planted outside (above).

Start broccoli indoors if you have a short growing season (below).

Place smaller seeds in a folded piece of paper and sprinkle evenly over the soil. Mix tiny seeds with fine sand and sprinkle on the soil surface. Follow seed packet instructions for planting depth.

While seeds are germinating, place pots or flats in plastic bags to retain humidity. Many planting trays come with clear plastic covers that keep in moisture. Once seeds germinate, remove the cover.

Water seeds and small seedlings gently with a fine spray from a hand-held mister—a strong spray can easily wash small seeds away.

Seeds provide all the energy and nutrients that young seedlings require. Small seedlings do not need to be fertilized until they have about four or five true leaves. When the first leaves begin to shrivel, the plant has used up all its seed energy, and you can use a fertilizer diluted to quarter strength.

If seedlings get too big for their containers before you're ready to plant, move them to slightly larger container to avoid confining the roots. Before placing them in the garden, harden plants off by leaving them outdoors for longer periods every day over a week.

When you plant seeds directly into the garden, the procedure is similar. Begin with a well-prepared, smoothly raked bed. The small furrows left by the rake help hold moisture and prevent seeds from being washed away. Sprinkle the seeds onto the soil and cover them lightly with peat moss or more soil. To ensure even germination, keep the soil moist using a gentle spray. Cover your newly seeded bed with chicken wire, an old sheet or some thorny branches to discourage pets from digging.

Large seeds are easy to see, sow and plant. Small seeds are a little trickier; because it's harder to determine placement, you may need to thin crops as they emerge. Pull out the weaker plants when groups look crowded. Use the edible thinnings from lettuce, spinach and others in a salad or stir-fry.

Vegetables for Direct Seeding

Beans	Corn
Beets	Lettuce
Carrots	Peas
Chard	Radishes

Growing Vegetables

No matter where you live in California, homegrown vegetables are tasty and rewarding. Kids often love to help garden and gain extra knowledge and nutrition in the process. Cooks and non-cooks alike take great delight in presenting a dish and saying, "I grew that in my garden!" Figure out what you and your family like to eat, and get growing!

Planting

Once your plants have hardened off, it is time to plant them out. If your beds are already prepared, you are ready to start. The only tool you are likely to need is a trowel. Set aside enough time to complete the job; young plants will dry and die if left out in the sun. Try to choose an overcast day for planting.

When you're ready to plant, the only tool you'll need is a trowel.

Use your trowel to make a planting hole.

garden, remove the top 1½ to 2½ inches of the pot. If any of the pot is sticking up out of the soil, it can wick moisture away from your plant.

Holding the plant in one hand, insert your trowel into the soil and pull it toward you, creating a wedge. Place your plant into the hole and firm the soil around it with your hands. Water gently but thoroughly. Until it is established, the plant will need regular watering.

Some of the plants in this book are sold in large containers. In a prepared bed, dig a hole that will accommodate the rootball. Fill the hole in gradually, settling the soil with water as you go.

Other plants are sold as bare roots or crowns, or in moistened peat moss, sphagnum moss or sawdust. Shake off any packing material and soak these plants for a few hours before planting. Be sure to accommodate the roots; spread them out in a hole big enough to hold them without crowding.

Plants are easier to remove from their containers if the soil is moist. Push on the bottom of the cell to ease them out. If roots have grown together, free them by gently untangling by hand or immersing them in water and washing away some of the soil. If you must handle the plant, hold it by a leaf to avoid crushing the stem. Remove and discard any damaged leaves or growth.

The rootball should contain a network of white plant roots. If the rootball is densely matted and twisted, break the tangles apart with your thumbs. New root growth will start from the breaks, allowing the plant to spread outward.

Plants started in peat pots and peat pellets can be planted pot and all. When planting peat pots into the

A few plants are sold as bulbs, such as garlic and onion sets. Plant these about three times as deep as the bulb is high.

More detailed planting instructions are given, as needed, in the plant accounts.

Mulching

Until recently, no one said much about mulch. Now it's all the rage with California gardeners who have discovered mulch's ability to keep the soil moist and maintain consistent soil temperatures. In areas that receive heavy wind or rainfall, mulch protects soil and prevents erosion. Put a layer around your plants to reduce weed germination.

Effective in beds, planters and containers, mulches come in many varieties. Organic mulches such as compost, grass clippings or shredded leaves add nutrients as they break down. They improve the quality of the soil and, ultimately, the health of your plants. Avoid colored mulch or large chunks of bark; these decompose slowly, if at all, and may contain chemicals that will not help your soil.

Spread about 2 to 4 inches of mulch over the soil after you have finished planting, or spread your mulch first and then make spaces to plant afterward. Don't pile it near plant stems and crowns, where it will harm your plants by trapping moisture, preventing air circulation and encouraging fungal disease. Replenish your mulch as it breaks down.

A straw mulch will benefit your vegetable plants, including kale (above) and zucchini (below).

Weeds are not all bad. Some provide benefits to the garden. Deeply rooted weeds bring nutrients to the surface, making them available for your vegetable plants, and help to aerate the soil and prevent soil erosion. Many weeds are sources of food for beneficial insects. Clover, milkweed, nettles, thistles, chickweed, wild mustard and Queen Anne's lace are all attractive to organisms that will benefit your garden.

Clover can be beneficial, so leave it alone unless it begins to crowd out companions like this squash.

One tip for weed prevention is to not bring weeds into your garden, either in newly purchased transplants, on your shoes or on your tools. Make sure your tools are clean before using them in the garden.

Underneath this glorious mulch, the earthworms do their job by aerating the soil and producing castings, a product that is priceless to the soil and your plants. They will also do the job of pulling the nutrients from the compost and decomposing mulch further down in the soil around the root zone of the plants, leaving you with more time to enjoy the fruits (or vegetables) of your labor.

Weeding

Controlling weeds keeps the garden healthy and neat. Weeds compete for light, nutrients and space, and they can also harbor pests and diseases.

Pull weeds by hand or hoe. The best time is shortly after it rains, when soil is soft and damp. Try to pull weeds while they are still small. Once they are large enough to flower, many will quickly set seed; then you will have an entire new generation to worry about.

It can be a little daunting to witness the vigor and aggressiveness of weeds. The first step in weed prevention is understanding how weeds start in the first place. Millions of seeds are present in the soil, aside from the ones that blow in from other locations. The seeds in the soil are able to produce an annual crop for a minimum of nine years, and longer for the more persistent species. All they require to germinate is light. Every time the soil is disturbed, be it from digging, tilling or even walking on it, more seeds are exposed and the germination rate is increased exponentially. Adapt by turning the garden as little as possible. Instead, use a deep-dig method by preparing the garden soil more thoroughly at the beginning of the season. Only the topsoil should be dug thoroughly and broken up into smaller pieces, followed by additions of compost and other soil amendments. Then comes resisting the temptation to dig, hoe and till time and time again to reduce the weed population, when in fact you're only encouraging it.

Watering

Due to a severe water shortage throughout much of the state, California gardeners are learning to be water smart. That means using efficient tools such as drip watering systems and moisture meters. To conserve water and grow healthy plants, water when your plants need it—not when you get around to it. Automated systems have many advantages, but they are no substitute for personally checking individual plants on an ongoing basis. Just make it part of your weeding, deadheading and produce-picking routine.

Whenever possible, avoid wetting leaves. Wet leaves, fruit and vegetables attract fungal and other diseases. Keep the moisture at the base of the plant.

Timing is important, too. The best time to water is always early in the morning, whether it's manually, by sprinkler or by soaker hose. The plants then have time to dry off before the sun is at its hottest, while the moist soil keeps them cool for as long as possible into the day. Early morning watering also reduces evaporation, which results in less water used and wasted. Use mulch

Recycle an old, leaky hose; turn it into a soaker or drip hose. Simply poke holes into the hose every few inches and use it just as you would use one designed for such a purpose.

Use a soaker hose to apply water directly to the soil, reducing evaporation.

to prevent water from evaporating out of the soil.

All plants have different watering requirements, and those are spelled out in the individual listings. Many of them appreciate thorough but infrequent irrigation to develop deep roots. In a dry spell, they will seek out water trapped deep in the ground. Those that get a light daily sprinkle develop roots that stay close to the soil surface, making the plants vulnerable to heat.

Other plants have roots that naturally stay close to the surface. They will need more frequent water to keep the roots from drying out. For greatest efficiency, plant deep-rooted and shallow-rooted plants near companions with similar requirements.

To save time, money and water, you may wish to install an irrigation system, which applies the water exactly where it is needed: near the roots. Drip irrigation is as simple as a soaker hose set on the soil among the plants and hooked up to a water source. A timer can also be applied for regular, measured watering. A drip system has several advantages:

- quantity of water used is much less than with conventional methods

- moisture is applied almost directly to the roots, slowly, resulting in better penetration

- the soil is watered more evenly and thoroughly

- less effort is spent in moving hoses and equipment because you do it less often.

Consult with your local garden center or landscape professionals for more information.

Plants in containers, hanging baskets and planters need watering more frequently than in-ground plants—even twice daily during hot, sunny weather. The smaller the container, the more often the plants will need water.

Fertilizing

We demand a lot from our vegetable plants. Many are annuals, and we expect them to grow and produce a good crop of fruit or vegetables in only one season. They, in return, demand a lot of sun, nutrients and water. Mixing plenty of compost into the soil is a good start, but fertilizing regularly can make a big difference when it comes time to harvest your crop.

Whenever possible, use organic fertilizers. They do double duty by feeding your plants and improving your soil. They are non-toxic and will not harm the microorganisms in your soil. Synthetic fertilizers give plants a quick boost but deplete soil. There are many safe, non-toxic fertilizers such as fish emulsion, rock dusts, seaweed, compost, composted manure and compost tea. Find them online or at your local garden center, or, in the case of compost tea, make it yourself.

Organic and synthetic fertilizer comes in many forms. Liquids or water-soluble powders are easiest to use when watering. Slow-release pellets or granules are mixed into the garden or potting soil or are sprinkled around the plant.

Follow the directions carefully when using any fertilizer—using too much can kill your plants by burning their roots and may upset the soil's microbial balance, allowing pathogens to move in or dominate.

Compost or manure tea is one of the easiest and best forms of fertilizer. Simply put well-seasoned manure or compost into a burlap sack or old pillow case, tie at the top, attach to a strong stick or rod and dunk into a vessel of rainwater (treated water can be used but needs to be left for a day or two in the sun for the chemicals to dissipate before adding the living compost). Let it steep for a couple of hours or days. A shorter period is better because the microbe population starts decreasing if left too long, and you will want to use the tea when it has the highest microbe count. You are creating a fertilizer concentrate. The tea, if super fresh, can be used immediately and without diluting, either as a foliar spray or as a drench simply by pouring it into the soil. When steeped for longer periods, such as a day or two, dilute it by half before using it to water your plants. You can apply the tea weekly, or as infrequently as monthly. For foliar disease prevention, spray the plants just before disease usually occurs. Then spray every 10 to 14 days for about a month.

Compost tea aids in suppressing diseases that can affect your vegetable plants, such as black spot, downy mildew and Verticillium *wilt.*

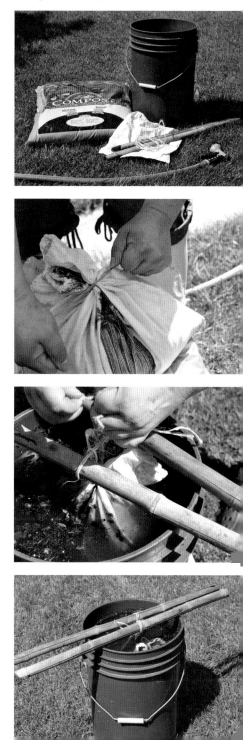

Making compost tea (all below)

Extending the Growing Season

There are ways to protect plants to extend your growing season by days, weeks, even months. Methods include cold frames, cloches and greenhouses.

For some California gardeners, frost is the enemy that curtails their growing season. Even in southern California, where frost is not a problem, some gardeners like to get a jump on the season by starting seedlings early so they can pop them into the ground as soon as possible.

Cold air tends to move downward to the lowest point, following the slopes in hills, walls and so on. The cool air will pool around anything that prevents it from moving any farther, such as a grouping of plants or a structure. Plants are better prepared to ward off any exposure to early-season cold air or frost if they've been hardened off. Harden off plants started indoors by gradually acclimating them to outside conditions by setting them in a sheltered location outdoors for increasing lengths of time over a period of days.

Cold frames are used to protect young plants grown from seeds or cuttings. A cold frame is a small wooden structure with a slanted glass or Plexiglas lid, often built very close to the ground, that acts like a mini greenhouse by allowing the sunlight to penetrate for plant growth and to heat the inside of the structure. The top is built to open fully for access to the plants, but it can also be opened just slightly throughout the day to prevent the plants from becoming too warm and to slowly harden off the plants inside to the temperatures outside.

Use a cold frame to protect seedlings.

Cloches serve the same purpose as cold frames and can be lifted slightly on one side during the day, allowing the plant to gradually acclimate to the surrounding air temperatures. While cold frames protect groups of plants, cloches protect individuals. They are often bell-shaped and made of blown, thickened glass for longevity, but plastic versions are much less expensive and easier to store. A great resource for the construction of cloches is the plastic bottle; simply cut the bottom from a plastic water or soda bottle and place the bottle over top of the seedling. The lid can be left on at night and removed during the day, allowing the air to move freely in and out while the plant acclimates to outside temperatures. Later on the neck of the bottle can be cut away, leaving only a plastic cylinder around the base of the plant to protect it from chewing insects as well as to act as a support throughout the growing season. Or the bottle can be taken away altogether.

Greenhouses are expensive but, for some gardeners, worth the money. With a greenhouse, regardless of size, you can extend your season by weeks or months, or you can just garden year-round. A greenhouse provides the best protection from the outdoor elements and is invaluable to gardeners in regions with short summers and cold winters. Plants can be raised from seed to maturity, regardless of the time of year, or they can be started in the greenhouse and moved to cold frames before they're planted outdoors for the duration of the growing season.

Harvesting

Each plant featured in this book will have suggestions about when to harvest, but here are a few general tips.

Make a list of the maturity dates for the vegetable plants you're growing. Once the time allowance has been met, observe the vegetables to see if they're ready to be harvested. Don't harvest too early or too late. Vegetables picked earlier than necessary

To enjoy corn at its best, don't pick it too early or too late.

are often bland, hard and small. Veggies that are left too long are often bland, tough and stringy. Only trial and error will teach you the perfect time to harvest, but observe and taste your produce and record your findings to better prepare for the following growing season.

For the best culinary experience, try to harvest right before preparing, cooking or eating the produce to get the full benefit of the flavor and nutrients. However, if you're planning on storing the produce, particularly leafy vegetables, for any length of time, harvest early in morning when dew is left behind on the leaves.

Use sharp, clean tools when harvesting vegetables. Some plants can be damaged when the fruit is pulled rather than cut off with a sharp tool, which may result in a plant that is no longer able to produce. Pulling on a tomato and snapping your tomato plant in half early on will be the season's biggest disappointment, particularly because it could have been prevented.

There are many more tips and tricks to learn that will help you, not only throughout the growing phase of vegetables but also during the harvest. The foregoing are only the basics. Strike up a conversation with friends, family and neighbors who garden, and you'll soon find that some of their tried-and-true methods will become part of your seasonal routine.

Harvesting throughout the season is the best reward for all of your hard work.

Guide to Pests and Diseases

New annual vegetable plants are planted each spring and fall, and you may choose to plant different species each year. Changing and adding new varieties makes it difficult for pests and diseases to find their preferred host plants and establish a population. However, because many edibles are closely related, any problems are likely to attack all the plants in the same family. Pests that love your broccoli will also be enamored of your cauliflower, for example.

For many years, pest control meant spraying or dusting with the goal of eliminating every pest in the landscape. Today's more moderate approach is IPM (Integrated Pest Management or Integrated Plant Management), a sort of live-and-let-live policy. The goal of IPM is to reduce pest problems so only negligible damage is done. Of course, you must determine what degree of damage is acceptable to you. Consider whether a pest's damage is localized or covers the entire plant. Will the damage kill the plant or is it affecting only the outward appearance? Are there methods of controlling the pest without chemicals?

A good IPM program includes learning about the conditions your plants need for healthy growth, which pests might affect your plants, where and when to look for those pests and how to control them. Keep records of pest damage because your observations can reveal patterns useful in spotting recurring problems and in planning your maintenance regime.

All plants in the Brassica family, including Brussels sprouts, are somewhat prone to pests and diseases.

There are four steps in effective and responsible pest management. Cultural controls are the most important and are the first response when problems arise. Use physical controls next, followed by biological controls. Resort to chemical controls only when the first three possibilities have been exhausted. Even then, consider that there may be other alternatives. It's worthwhile to do a little research before applying a synthetic, chemical pesticide.

Cultural controls are simply the day-to-day techniques you use to care for your garden. Keeping your plants as healthy as possible is the best defense against pests. Growing plants in the conditions they prefer and keeping your soil healthy by adding plenty of organic matter are just two of the cultural controls you can use to keep pests manageable. Choose disease-resistant varieties to minimize problems. Space plants to provide good air circulation and to reduce stress caused by competition for light, nutrients and space. Take plants that are destroyed by the same pests every year out of the landscape. Remove diseased foliage and branches, and burn or take them to a permitted dumpsite. Prevent the spread of disease by keeping gardening tools clean and by tidying up fallen leaves and dead plant matter at the end of every growing season.

Physical controls are generally used to combat insect problems. They include picking the insects off by hand, using barriers, and installing traps that catch or confuse them. Physical control of disease may require removing the infected plant or plant part to keep the problem from spreading.

Biological controls use predators that prey on pests. Animals such as birds, snakes, frogs, spiders and lady beetles, as well as certain bacteria, can play an important role in keeping pest populations manageable. Encourage these creatures to take up permanent residence in your garden. A birdbath and birdfeeder will make birds more likely to enjoy your yard and feed on a wide variety of insect pests. Many beneficial insects are probably already living in your landscape, and you can encourage

Lady beetle larva

Lady beetle (above)

them to stay by planting appropriate food sources. Herbs such as parsley, thyme and oregano attract beneficial insects.

Chemical controls should rarely be necessary, but if you must use them, there are some organic options available. Both organic and synthetic chemical sprays are dangerous, but organics break down into harmless compounds. Traditional chemicals linger in the garden and may have long-lasting negative effects. Both organic and traditional chemicals may also kill the beneficial insects you have been trying to attract to your garden.

Use IPM techniques to maintain a healthy garden (below).

Organic chemicals are available at most garden centers.

Follow the manufacturer's instructions carefully. A large amount of pesticide is no more effective than the recommended amount. Note that if a particular pest is not listed on the package, that product will not control that pest. Proper and early identification of pests is vital to finding a quick solution.

Cultural, physical, biological and chemical controls provide defense against insects, but until recently, diseases could only be controlled culturally. New organic products promise to protect susceptible plants from some diseases. Still, the best plan is to garden smart and attempt to keep diseases from gaining hold. Not surprisingly, healthy plants often fight off illness, though some diseases can infect plants regardless of their level of health. Prevention is key. Once a plant has been infected, you may have to destroy it to prevent the disease from spreading.

The Pests and Diseases

Anthracnose

Fungus. Yellow or brown spots on leaves; sunken lesions and blisters on stems; can kill plant.

What to do: choose resistant varieties and cultivars; keep soil well drained; thin out stems to improve air circulation; avoid handling wet foliage; remove and destroy infected plant parts; clean up and destroy debris from infected plants at end of growing season.

Aphids

Insects. Tiny, pear-shaped, green, black, brown, red or gray; can be winged or wingless, e.g., woolly adelgids. Cluster along stems, on buds and on leaves; suck sap from plant; cause distorted or stunted growth; sticky honeydew forms on plant surfaces and encourages sooty mold growth.

What to do: squish small colonies by hand; dislodge with brisk water spray;

Aphids

encourage predatory insects and birds that feed on aphids; spray serious infestations with insecticidal soap or neem oil according to package directions.

Aster Yellows

see Viruses

Beetles

Insects; many types. Usually rounded with hard, shell-like outer wings covering membranous inner wings; vary in size. Some are beneficial, e.g., ladybird beetles ("ladybugs"); others, e.g., Japanese beetles, leaf skeletonizers and weevils, eat plants. Leave wide range of chewing damage: make small or large holes in or around margins of leaves; consume entire leaves or areas between leaf veins ("skeletonize"); may also chew holes in flowers. Some bark beetle species carry deadly plant diseases. Larvae: *see* Borers; Grubs.

What to do: pick beetles off at night and drop them into an old coffee can half filled with soapy water (soap prevents them from floating and climbing out).

Blight

Fungal diseases; many types, e.g., leaf blight, needle blight, snow blight. Leaves, stems and flowers blacken, rot and die.

What to do: remove and destroy infected plant parts; thin stems to improve air circulation; keep mulch away from base of plants; remove debris from garden at end of growing season.

Colorado potato beetle

Borers

Larvae of some moths, wasps and beetles; among the most damaging plant pests. Worm-like; vary in size and get bigger as they bore through plants. Burrow into plant stems, branches, leaves and/or roots; destroy vascular tissue (plant veins and arteries) and structural strength. May see tunnels in leaves, stems or roots; stems weaken and may break; leaves will wilt; rhizomes may be hollowed out entirely or in part.

What to do: may be able to squish borers within leaves; remove and destroy bored parts; may need to dig up and destroy infected roots and rhizomes.

Bugs (True Bugs)

Insects; many are beneficial, but a few are pests. Green, brown, black or brightly colored and patterned; up to ½ inch long. Pierce plants to suck out sap; toxins may be injected that deform plants.

Sunken areas remain where pierced; leaves rip as they grow; leaves, buds and new growth may be dwarfed and deformed.

What to do: remove debris and weeds from around plants in fall to destroy overwintering sites. Spray plants with insecticidal soap or neem oil according to package directions.

Case Bearers

see Caterpillars

Caterpillars

Larvae of butterflies, moths and saw-flies; include bagworms, budworms, case bearers, cutworms, leaf rollers, leaf tiers, loopers. Chew foliage and buds; can completely defoliate a plant if infestation is severe.

What to do: removal from plant is best control; use high-pressure water and soap or pick caterpillars off by hand. Control biologically using the naturally occurring soil bacterium

Borer damage

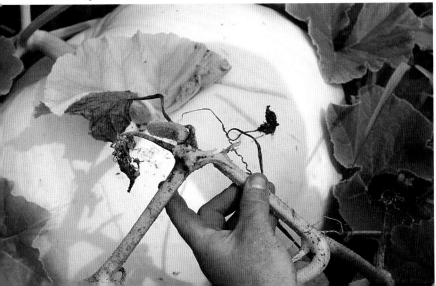

Bacillus thuringiensis var. *kurstaki* or B.t.k. (commercially available), which breaks down the gut lining of caterpillars.

Cutworms

see Caterpillars

Deer

Can decimate crops, woodlands and gardens; can kill saplings by rubbing their antlers on the trees, girdling the bark or snapping the trees in two; host ticks that carry Lyme disease and Rocky Mountain spotted fever.

What to do: many deterrents work for a while: encircle immature shrubs with tall, upright sticks; place dangling soap bars around the garden; use noisemaking devices or water spritzers to startle deer; mount flashy aluminum or moving devices throughout the garden.

Galls

Unusual swellings of plant tissues that may be caused by insects or diseases. Can affect leaves, buds, stems, flowers, fruit; often a specific gall affects a single genus or species.

What to do: cut galls out of plant and destroy them. A gall caused by an insect usually contains the insect's eggs and juvenile stages; prevent such galls by controlling the insect before it lays eggs; otherwise try to remove and destroy infected tissue before young insects emerge; insect galls are generally more unsightly than damaging to plant. Galls caused by diseases often require destruction of plant; don't place other plants susceptible to same disease in that location.

Gray Mold

see Blight

Galls

Grubs

Larvae of different beetles. White or gray body; head may be white, gray, brown or reddish; usually curled in C-shape; commonly found below soil level. Problematic in lawns; may feed on roots of perennials. Plant wilts despite regular watering; may pull easily out of ground in severe cases.

What to do: toss grubs onto a stone path, driveway, road or patio for birds to devour; apply parasitic nematodes or milky spore to infested soil (ask at your local garden center).

Leafhoppers and Treehoppers

Insects. Small, wedge-shaped; can be green, brown, gray or multi-colored; jump around frantically when disturbed. Suck juice from plant leaves; cause distorted growth; carry diseases such as aster yellows.

What to do: encourage predators by planting nectar-producing species such as coriander. Wash insects off with strong spray of water; spray with insecticidal soap or neem oil according to package directions.

Leaf Miners

Larvae of some butterflies and moths. Tiny, stubby; yellow or green. Tunnel within leaves, leaving winding trails; tunneled areas lighter in color than rest of leaf. Unsightly rather than major health risk to plant.

What to do: remove debris from area in fall to destroy overwintering sites; attract parasitic wasps with nectar plants such as yarrow and

Leaf miner damage

coriander; remove and destroy infected foliage; can sometimes squish larvae by hand within leaf.

Leaf Rollers

see Caterpillars

Leaf Skeletonizers

see Beetles

Leaf Spot

Two common types: one caused by bacteria, the other by fungi. Bacterial: small brown or purple spots grow to encompass entire leaves; leaves may drop. Fungal: black, brown or yellow spots; leaves wither; e.g., scab, tar spot.

What to do: Bacterial: infection is more severe, must remove entire plant. Fungal: remove and destroy infected plant parts; sterilize removal tools; avoid wetting foliage or touching wet foliage; remove and destroy debris at end of growing season.

Maggots

Larvae of several species of flies (cabbage root maggots, carrot rust flies). Small; white or gray; worm-like. Tunnel into roots of a variety of plants, including many root vegetables. Stunt plants and disfigure roots; serious infestations can kill plants.

What to do: use floating row covers to prevent flies from laying eggs near roots. Apply parasitic nematodes to soil around plants. Use an early crop of radishes as a trap crop; pull them up and destroy them as soon as they become infested with maggots.

Root maggots on radishes

Mealybugs

Insects; related to aphids. Tiny; appear to be covered with white fuzz or flour. Sucking damage stunts and stresses plant; excrete honeydew that promotes growth of sooty mold.

What to do: remove by hand from smaller plants; wash plant with soap and water or wipe with

Mealybugs (above)

Powdery mildew (below)

alcohol-soaked swabs; spray with insecticidal soap; remove heavily infested leaves. Encourage or introduce natural predators such as mealybug destroyer beetles and parasitic wasps. Larvae of mealybug destroyer beetles look like very large mealybugs.

Mice

Burrow under mulch in winter, chewing plant roots, bark, bulbs and many other underground goodies; even plants or roots stored in cool porches, garages or sheds are fair game.

What to do: fine wire mesh can prevent mice from getting at your plants in winter, though they are quite ingenious and may find their way through or around any barrier you erect; roll bulbs and lifted roots in talcum powder, garlic powder or bulb protectant spray before storing or planting. Get a cat, or borrow your neighbor's, if you must.

Mildew

Two types, both caused by fungus, but with slightly different symptoms. Downy mildew: yellow spots on upper sides of leaves and downy fuzz on undersides; fuzz may be yellow, white or gray. Powdery mildew: white or gray, powdery coating on leaf surfaces that doesn't brush off.

What to do: choose resistant cultivars; space plants well; thin stems to encourage air circulation; tidy any debris in fall; remove and destroy infected parts. Spray weekly with mix of 1 part skim milk, 9 parts water. Use only skim milk because it contains an enzyme that fights mildew.

Spider mite web

Mites

Eight-legged relatives of spiders; e.g., bud mites, spider mites, spruce mites. Tiny, almost invisible to naked eye; red, yellow or green. Do not eat insects, but may spin webs; usually found on undersides of plant leaves; may see fine webbing on leaves and stems or mites moving on leaf undersides. Suck juice out of leaves; leaves become discolored and speckled, then turn brown and shrivel up.

What to do: wash off with strong spray of water daily until all signs of infestation are gone; spray plants with insecticidal soap. Predatory mites are available through garden centers.

Moles and Gophers

Burrow under the soil, tunneling throughout your property in search of insects, grubs and earthworms; tunnels can create runways for voles that will eat your plants from below ground.

What to do: castor oil (the primary ingredient in most repellents made to thwart moles and gophers) spilled down the mole's runway is effective and is available in granulated pellet form, too; noisemakers and predator urine are also useful; humane trapping is effective, as is having a cat or dog.

Mosaic

see Viruses

Nematodes

Tiny worms that give plants disease symptoms; one type infects foliage and stems, the other infects roots. Foliar: leaves have yellow spots that turn brown; leaves shrivel and wither; problem starts on lowest leaves and works up plant. Root-knot: plant is stunted and may wilt; yellow spots on leaves; roots have tiny bumps or knots.

What to do: mulch soil; add organic matter; clean up debris in fall; don't touch wet foliage of infected plants. Can add parasitic nematodes to soil; remove infected plants in extreme cases.

Rabbits

Can eat as much of your garden as deer and munch on the bark of trees and shrubs.

What to do: deterrents that work for deer usually keep rabbits away, as will humane trapping; having a cat or dog patrol your garden may also be effective.

Neem oil is the oil of the Indian neem tree, used in dilute form to kill bugs. Neem is a natural insecticide and will disable both beneficial and harmful insects.

Raccoons

Are especially fond of fruit and some vegetables; can carry rabies and canine distemper; also eat grubs, insects and mice, so can sometimes be helpful to gardeners.

What to do: don't allow access to garbage or pet food. Humane traps and relocation are best solutions; call your local SPCA or Humane Society to relocate individuals.

Rot

Several different fungi that affect different parts of plant, sometimes even killing it. Crown rot: affects base of plant; stems blacken and fall over; leaves turn yellow and wilt. Root rot: leaves turn yellow and wilt; digging up plant shows roots rotted away. White rot: a "watery decay fungus" that affects any part of plant; cell walls appear to break down, releasing fluids.

What to do: keep soil well drained; don't damage plant if you are digging around it; keep mulches away

Rust

from plant base; destroy infected plant if whole plant is affected.

Rust

Fungi; e.g., blister rust, hollyhock rust. Pale spots on upper leaf surfaces; orange, fuzzy or dusty spots on leaf undersides.

What to do: choose rust-resistant varieties and cultivars; avoid handling wet leaves; provide plant with good air circulation; clear up garden debris at end of season; remove and destroy infected plant parts.

Scab

see Leaf Spot

Scale Insects

Tiny, shelled insects. Suck sap, weakening and possibly killing plant or making it vulnerable to other problems; once female scale insect has pierced plant with mouthpart, it is there for life. Juvenile scale insects are called crawlers.

What to do: wipe bugs off with alcohol-soaked swabs; spray plant with water to dislodge crawlers; prune out heavily infested branches. Encourage natural predators and parasites; spray dormant oil in spring before bud break.

Slugs and Snails

Slugs lack shells; snails have a spiral shell; both have slimy, smooth skin; can be up to 8 inches long but are usually much smaller; gray, green, black, beige, yellow or spotted. Leave large, ragged holes in leaves

Slug (above)

Snail (below)

and silvery slime trails on and around plants.

What to do: attach strips of copper to wood around raised beds or smaller boards inserted around susceptible groups of plants (slugs and snails get shocked if they touch copper surfaces); pick off by hand in evening and squish or drop in a can of soapy water; spread wood ash or diatomaceous earth (available in garden centers) around plants (it pierces their soft bodies and causes them to dehydrate); use slug baits containing iron phosphate, which will not harm humans or pets. If slugs caused damage last season, begin controls as soon as new green shoots appear in spring.

Sooty Mold

Fungus. Thin, black film forms on leaf surfaces and reduces amount of light getting to leaf surfaces.

What to do: wipe mold off leaves; control aphids, mealybugs and whiteflies (honeydew left on leaves encourages mold).

Squirrels

Unearth and eat bulbs and corms, as well as flowers, fruits and vegetables; hone their teeth on almost everything else; raid birdfeeders and often eat the feeder itself; bury their food for later consumption, which can result in seeds germinating and plants springing up where you never wanted them.

What to do: cut heavy metal screening (hardware cloth) to fit around the plant stem; caging entire plants is effective if you don't mind your garden looking like a zoo; removing enticing food supplies is effective, but often impractical; trapping and moving is one option but usually results in other squirrels moving in.

Squirrel

Tar Spot

see Leaf Spot

Thrips

Insects. Tiny, slender; yellow, black or brown; narrow, fringed wings; difficult to see but may be visible if you disturb them by blowing gently on an infested flower. Suck juice out of plant cells, particularly in flowers and buds; cause mottled petals and leaves, dying buds and distorted and stunted growth.

What to do: remove and destroy infected plant parts; encourage native predatory insects with nectar plants like yarrow or coriander; spray severe infestations with insecticidal soap or neem oil according to package directions.

Viruses

Include aster yellows, mosaic virus and ringspot virus. Plant may be stunted and leaves and flowers distorted, streaked or discolored.

Mosaic virus

What to do: new organic sprays such as Serenade show promise in fighting viral diseases in plants. Control disease-spreading insects, such as aphids, leafhoppers and whiteflies. If disease is widespread, destroy infected plants.

Voles

Mouse-like creatures. Damage plants at or just beneath the soil surface; mostly herbivorous, feeding on a variety of grasses, herbaceous plants, bulbs (lilies are a favorite) and tubers; also eat bark and roots of trees, usually in fall or winter; store seeds and other plant matter in underground chambers.

What to do: wire fences at least 12 inches tall with a mesh size of ½ inch or less and buried 6–8 inches deep can help exclude voles from gardens; fence can either stand alone or be attached to the bottom of an existing fence; a weed-free barrier outside fence will increase effectiveness. Burrow fumigants do not effectively control voles because the vole's burrow system is shallow and has many open holes;

Use a pheremone trap to monitor insect populations.

electromagnetic or ultrasonic devices and flooding are also ineffective. When vole populations are not numerous or are concentrated in a small area, trapping may be effective; use enough traps to control the population: for a small garden use at least 12 traps, and for larger areas 50 or more may be needed. A dog or cat is a deterrent. Do not use poisonous repellents or baits if your pets or children romp around the garden.

Weevils

see Beetles

Whiteflies

Insects. Tiny, white, moth-like; flutter up into the air when plant is disturbed; live on undersides of plant leaves. Suck juice out of leaves, causing yellowed leaves and weakened plants; leave behind sticky honeydew on leaves, encouraging sooty mold growth.

What to do: destroy weeds where insects may live; attract native predatory beetles and parasitic wasps with nectar plants like yarrow or coriander; spray severe cases with insecticidal soap. Can make a sticky flypaper-like trap by mounting a tin can on a stake, wrapping can with yellow paper and covering it with a clear plastic bag smeared with petroleum jelly; replace bag when covered in flies.

Wilt

If watering doesn't help wilted plants, one of two wilt fungi may be to blame. *Fusarium* wilt: plant wilts; leaves turn

yellow then die; symptoms generally appear first on one part of plant before spreading to other parts. *Verticillium* wilt: plant wilts; leaves curl up at edges; leaves turn yellow then drop off; plant may die.

What to do: both wilts are difficult to control; choose resistant plant varieties and cultivars; clean up debris at end of growing season. Destroy infected plants; solarize (sterilize) soil before replanting (may help if entire bed of plants lost to these fungi)—contact local garden center for assistance. New organic sprays such as Serenade can help prevent wilts when applied early and consistently.

Woolly Adelgids

see Aphids

Worms

see Caterpillars, Nematodes

Homemade Insecticidal Soap

❁ 1 tsp mild dish detergent or pure soap (biodegradable options are available)

❁ 4 cups water

Mix in a clean spray bottle and spray the surfaces of your plants. Rinse well within an hour to avoid foliage discoloration.

About this Guide

The plants featured in this book are organized alphabetically by their most familiar common names. Additional common names appear as well. This system enables you to find a plant easily if you are familiar with only the common name. The scientific or botanical name is always listed after the common name. Why bother to learn the botanical name? To avoid confusion and ensure that you get what you want. Several plants may share the same common name, and other common names vary from region to region. Only the specific botanical name identifies the specific plant anywhere in the world.

Each entry gives clear instructions for planting and growing the plants, and recommends many favorite selections. In reference to spacing while planting or sowing seed, a plant's height and spread ranges are listed as general guidelines, but gardening intensively will reduce space requirements somewhat. All outstanding features are described in the recommended section of each vegetable account, particularly the unusual species, cultivars, hybrids and varieties. Your local garden center will have any additional information you need about the plant and will help you make your final plant selections.

Following the more traditional vegetable accounts is a grouping of herbs and flowers that will help your vegetable garden flourish and add flavor and color to your cooking.

Finally, refer back to the pests and diseases section of the introduction to learn about issues that may afflict your garden plants from time to time.

Artichokes
Globe Artichokes
Cynara

California produces nearly all artichokes grown in the United States. One of the few vegetables that thrive in foggy coastal areas, artichokes are grown commercially in the northern California town of Castroville, which has its own artichoke festival. They flourish in the San Francisco Bay area and in coastal southern California gardens. This Mediterranean thistle can spread to 6 feet, so plan accordingly! Fortunately, their unique architectural beauty makes these perennials welcome in the garden year-round.

Starting

In warm winter areas, direct seed in fall. Where winters are cool, start seeds indoors about 8–12 weeks before the last frost date. In both cases, plant to a depth of ¼ inch. Keep seeds moist with good drainage. Seeds germinate in about 10–20 days in warm soil. Frost and freezing temperatures can kill the plant, so don't rush. For an early yield, consider 'Imperial Star,' one of the only varieties to produce the first year.

Since artichokes are increasingly available in nurseries, transplants are a simple alternative. Water the soil first, then plant 6 inches deep. Keep the tops above ground level and water consistently and evenly, making sure soil is draining well. Water-starved chokes are less flavorful, yet over watering can be fatal.

With any luck, you and your artichoke will be together for several years, so plan your garden accordingly. Space plants about 6 feet apart.

Growing

Artichokes grow best in **full sun**, though they appreciate some afternoon shade in hotter locations. The soil should be **fertile, humus rich, moist** and **well drained**.

Harvest your first artichokes in spring. For a second crop, cut the plant to soil level and stop watering for several weeks. This forced dormancy may convince your artichoke to produce once again when you start watering in fall.

In cold winter areas, protect the plant with straw. Remove it only when danger of frost has passed.

Try to keep your artichoke going! The longer it grows, the more artichokes you'll harvest.

Ancient Greeks and Romans believed artichokes were aphrodisiacs.

Store unwashed artichokes in a sealed plastic bag in the refrigerator. Mist or sprinkle them with a bit of water to prevent dehydration. They will keep for up to 2 weeks.

'Green Globe' (below)

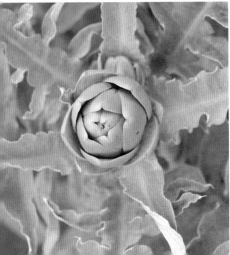

Harvesting

Artichokes produce one large flower bud on the central stalk and many smaller flower buds on the side shoots. The flower buds are rounded and made of tightly packed scales. They are usually ready for harvest when lemon-sized with slightly loose scales. With a sharp knife, cut about 4–6 inches below the bud base to encourage additional production of heads.

A cool-weather vegetable, artichokes produce most abundantly before the heat sets in. In cool-summer areas, you may get artichokes year-round.

Tips

Artichoke plants make dramatic additions to vegetable and ornamental gardens. If you resist eating the chokes, enjoy the huge purple flowers. At up to 7 inches across, these blossoms are stunning in fresh flower arrangements.

Recommended

C. scolymus forms a large clump of deeply lobed, pointy-tipped, gray-green leaves. It grows 2–7 feet tall and spreads 4–6 feet. In spring or sometimes fall, it bears large, scaled flower buds that open if not picked for eating. **'Green Globe'** is one of the most popular cultivars because it is tasty and is one of the quickest to mature and flower. **'Green Globe Improved'** does well in shorter seasons, has fewer spines and bears heavier fruit. It still requires 180–240 days to mature. **'Imperial Star'** is one of the easiest to grow from seed, being specifically bred for annual production, and is ideal for colder climates or shorter seasons. It will bear fruit in the first season from seed, producing 6–8 mature buds. **'Purple of Romagna'** is an Italian heirloom known for its tenderness and color. **'Tempo'** is mature at 100 days, purple in color and can be grown very successfully as an annual. **'Violetto'** is an Italian artichoke that produces purple heads. This variety takes longer to mature but is definitely worth the experiment.

Problems and Pests

Control snails and slugs with pet-friendly deterrents containing iron phosphate. Hose off aphids.

Monitor the heads as they develop. They'll become tough and woody if left too long.

Arugula
Roquette, Salad Rocket

Diplotaxis, Eruca

Easy to grow from seed, peppery arugula takes off like its alternate name: rocket. Mixed in with milder greens, it transforms a simple salad into something exotic. Some people consider this annual a vegetable, others an herb, and they're both right. Arugula is native to parts of Asia and southern Europe but has naturalized in parts of North America.

Starting

Start seeds in early spring and again in early fall, taking a break during summer heat. Within those periods, plant seeds in succession once or twice per week for a continuous supply of young, tender leaves. Plant only what you can harvest. The seed germinates quickly, sprouting in about a week. Arugula is known to self-seed prolifically, so you may only have to seed one season.

Growing

Arugula prefers **full sun** or **partial shade. Cool, moist, rich** soil will help produce more tender and less pungent leaves than will dry, hot soil. Pinch and use new leaves frequently. Excessive fertilizer results in lush leaves lacking flavor. Arugula can withstand light frosts.

Arugula is best grown in a vegetable or herb garden setting, in the ground, outdoors; however, it is possible to grow it in pots.

Harvesting

The leaves are aromatic, producing a peppery scent when harvested. They are best when picked tender, before flower stems emerge. Over time, they become more pungent and somewhat bitter. The leaves are ready for harvest 3–4 weeks after sowing and should always be used fresh, as drying them diminishes flavor.

For a great snack, toss arugula, olive oil and lemon pepper together and bake till crispy.

The flowers and seeds are also edible. The citrus-tasting flowers can be used as an edible garnish.

Tips

The leaves, though attractive, don't have much to offer in aesthetics. Arugula combines well with other herbs, including parsley, lovage, cilantro, basil, cress, dill, borage and salad burnet.

Add leaves to stir-fries, pasta sauces, potato salad or almost any dish where spinach is used. When used in salads, arugula is complemented by nutty oil dressings.

Recommended

D. tenuifolia (wild arugula) has a sharper flavor compared to the cultivated selections and is a favorite among chefs and cooks. It grows 12–14 inches tall. '**Discovery**' is a uniform, vigorous cultivar with an upright habit. It produces pungent leaves with a hint of sweetness in roughly 50 days from seed. '**Sylvetta**' is a perennial that grows into a very dense, small bush loaded with deeply lobed leaves. The flowers produced are also delicious.

You may come across a wild arugula that is completely different from the one recommended here. *D. muralis* is a perennial, producing more ornate leaves that are equally as pungent as those of *D. tenuifolia*. Turkish arugula (*Bunias orientalis*) produces leaves that resemble those of a dandelion.

The flavor of the leaves of both plants diminishes almost entirely once the flowers appear. They also become more peppery in flavor as they age, but only before flower production.

E. vesicaria **subsp. *sativa*** (salad arugula, salad rocket, roquette) is an upright annual with toothed leaves on tall stems tipped with 4-petaled, white flowers with purple veins, reminiscent of scented geranium flowers. This grouping of arugula is considered to be the cultivated selections, as opposed to the wild plants. Slender, erect seedpods follow the flowers. It can grow to 30 inches tall and 12 inches wide, but the flavor is best if leaves are harvested at 2–3 inches. '**Astro**' is ready for harvest in 38 days, producing a more mild flavor and rounded leaves. **'Runway'** is a vigorous grower, producing large, deeply lobed leaves. Harvest at 21 days for baby arugula. **'Surrey'** is mature in 21 days for baby leaves, 40 days for full-sized leaves. This late-bolting cultivar is rich and spicy.

Problems and Pests

Flea beetles, cutworms, aphids and thrips can all prey on arugula, but rarely, and they're all easily treatable with a sharp spray of water or an organic insecticidal soap. If you are concerned about pest problems, cover emerging plants with a floating row cover.

Arugula is popular in Mediterranean cuisine, as well as in herbal butters, dressings and pesto.

Asparagus

Asparagus

The large, ferny growth that asparagus develops comes as quite a surprise to first-time growers who may have seen only tidy bunches of spears at the grocery store. Asparagus is a member of the lily family, and well-established plants can last a lifetime, producing tasty spears every spring. This longevity is fortunate because this delicious vegetable takes a bit of work to get started.

Asparagus is dioecious—male and female flowers are borne on separate plants. Male plants are reputed to produce the greatest number of spears.

'Mary Washington'

Starting

Asparagus can be grown from seed, but it takes an average of 3 years before you get a full crop. Most people begin with 1-year-old crowns, or roots, purchased from the garden center. Start your crop from roots and you can harvest a year earlier.

Plant purchased roots in a well-prepared area. Work plenty of compost into the bed, then dig a trench or hole about 18 inches deep. Lay roots 18–24 inches apart from each other and other plants. Cover roots with 2–4 inches of soil and, as they sprout up, gradually cover them

with more soil until the trench or hole is filled. Water and mulch well.

Plant seeds indoors in flats or peat pots about 6–8 weeks before placing them in the garden. Use larger pots if seedlings get too big before you can move them outside. The first year, plant seedlings in the ground at the same soil level they experienced in pots. Keep them well watered and mulch with compost. The second season, the rooted seedlings can be planted, as described earlier, as roots or crowns in a trench.

The best time to plant is early winter to early spring—January through April. But if you're inland where summers

First-year plant (left); young 'Purple Passion' spears emerging (right)

are long and hot, plant in October through March.

Growing

Asparagus grows well in **full sun** or **partial shade** with protection from hot afternoon sun. The soil should be **fertile, humus rich, moist** and **well drained**. Apply a 4-inch layer of compost in spring and late summer. Weed regularly; this plant is most productive if it doesn't compete with other plants.

Harvesting

As mentioned, asparagus spears started from roots are ready for harvest 2 years after planting; spears started from seeds are ready in 3 years. Snap or cut spears off at ground level for about 4 weeks in spring and early summer. When new spears are thinner than a pencil, stop harvesting and let the plants grow in. Add a new layer of compost when you finish harvesting.

Stalks develop into shoots later in summer. Once they turn brown, cut them back. The spears will reappear next spring.

Tips

This hardy perennial plant is a welcome treat in spring and a beautiful addition to the back of a border.

Recommended

A. officinalis forms an airy mound of ferny growth. It grows 2–5 feet tall and spreads 2–4 feet. Small, white, summer flowers are followed by bright red berries, which can be collected for starting new plants. **'Jersey Giant'** is known for its high yield and production of the largest spears, while **'Jersey Knight'** produces premium quality spears nearly 1 inch thick. **'Jersey Supreme'** is known for its sheer abundance of spears produced once established. **'Martha Washington'** and **'Mary Washington'** are traditional, productive strains. **'Purple Passion'** produces sweet, tender spears, more so than green varieties. There is slightly lesser yield with this purple cultivar, however, because it is predominantly female. The purple spears turn green when cooked. **'Viking'** is one of the hardiest varieties available.

Problems and Pests

Rust can be a problem, so choose resistant cultivars. Clean up debris in fall to discourage asparagus beetles. If you discover them during the growing season, knock them off with a shot of water from the hose.

Asparagus has been a cultivated vegetable crop for over 2000 years. Popular with the Greeks, Romans and Egyptians, it also drew favor in the French court, where Louis XIV called it "the king of vegetables."

Beans

Phaseolus, Vicia

This incredibly diverse group of legumes is sure to please everyone; there are few things as delicious as fresh beans for dinner, straight out of the garden. Plants can be low or bushy, tall or twining. Delicious, versatile and ornamental, they are at home in a garden plot or rambling over a fence. The selection is almost endless.

Starting

Beans are quite possibly one of the easiest plants to grow from seed. The seeds are large and easy to handle and sprout quickly in warm, moist soil. Plant directly in the garden in warm soil after the last frost date. In mild winter areas, plant in late winter or spring. Plant seeds 4–8 inches apart.

Growing

Beans grow best in **full sun**, but tolerate some light afternoon shade. Plant in **average, well-drained** soil. Place the seeds in moist soil, then withhold water until seedlings appear; water consistently after that.

Bush beans are self-supporting, but climbing beans need a pole or trellis to grow up. The support structure should be in place at planting time to avoid disturbing the young plants or damaging their roots.

Beans can become less productive and look unattractive as summer wears on. Pull them up and plant something else in their place, or plant them with companions that mature more slowly to fill in the space left by the faded bean plants.

Harvesting

The most important thing to remember when harvesting beans is to do so only when the foliage is dry. Touching wet foliage encourages the spread of disease.

Different types of beans should be picked at different stages in their development. Green, runner, wax or snap beans are picked once the pod

Runner beans growing on a trellis (below)

is a good size but still young and tender. As they mature, they become stringy, woody and dry. Beans eaten as immature seeds, such as string beans, should be picked when pods are full and seeds are fleshy and moist. Keep picking! The more you pick, the more you'll get.

Beans for drying are left to mature on the plant. Once the plant begins to die back and before the seedpods open, cut the entire plant off at ground level (leave the roots to enrich the soil with nitrogen for other plants) and hang it upside down indoors to finish drying. You can then remove the beans from the pods and store them in airtight containers in a cool, dry place. The beans will keep for 10–12 months.

Tips

Beans are very ornamental, with attractive leaves and plentiful flowers. Climbing beans can grow up fences, trellises, obelisks and poles to create a screen or feature planting. Bush beans make low, temporary hedges or can be planted in small groups in a border.

Recommended

P. coccineus (runner bean) is a vigorous climbing plant with red or sometimes white or bicolored flowers. **'Scarlet Runner'** has bright red flowers and is one of the best and best-known cultivars. The beans can be eaten with the pod when they are young and tender, or the plants can be left to mature and the pink-and-purple-spotted beans can be dried. Plants produce edible beans in 70 days but need about 100 days for dry beans. **'Scarlet Empire'** is ready for harvest in 85 days, producing longer, smoother, stringless pods. **'Pantheon'** is another stringless selection. It is ready in 75 days and has flat, juicy pods 1 inch wide and 10 inches long. **'St. George'** is an award-winning selection that has smooth, fleshy pods 12 inches long. This early bean has good snap with little fiber when picked regularly.

P. lunatus (lima bean) may be climbing or bush, depending on the cultivar. The beans are eaten as immature seeds and should be picked when the pods are plump but the seeds are still tender. They take 70–85 days to mature. **'Fordhook'** is a popular bush variety, and **'King of the Garden'** is a good climbing selection with a tender, smooth texture.

P. vulgaris (wax bean, green bean, bush bean, pole bean, snap bean, dry bean) is probably the largest group of beans and includes bush beans and pole beans. Some are eaten immature in the pod, and others are grown to

Climbing beans are popular among gardeners with limited space because you can get more beans for less space. Legumes (including beans) are known for being able to fix nitrogen from the air into the soil through a symbiotic relationship with bacteria, which attach to the roots as small nodules. The bacteria turn the nitrogen from the air into useable nitrogen for the plant; in return, the plant feeds and supports the bacteria. The bacteria are present in most soils and are also available for purchase as an inoculant. Some bean seeds are also pre-treated with the bacteria.

maturity and used as dry beans. Bush bean cultivars include yellow **'Eureka'**; green, slim **'Jade'** and **'Rolande'**; and the unusually hued **'Purple Queen.'** Purple beans turn bright green when cooked. Bush beans take 50–60 days to mature.

Other interesting bush beans include the beautiful red-speckled **'Dwarf Barlotti,'** a 24-inch-tall plant with 6-inch-long pods. French-type **'Dwarf Delinel'** produces slender, light green pods at their best when picked about pencil-thick. **'Golden Roc d'Or'** is ready in 53 days and has a natural buttery flavor. This French gourmet bush bean is great for freezing and is a heavy yielder. **'Bush Blue Lake'** is a dwarf bush selection with dark bluish, 5- to 6-inch-long beans that are good for canning, freezing or eating fresh.

Pole beans, such as **'Blue Lake'** and **'Kentucky Blue,'** take 50–55 days to mature. Stringless **'Cobra'** grows to 6–8 feet tall and sports lovely purple flowers amid its straight 7-inch pods. Meaty, flat Romano type **'Helga'** grows 6–8 feet tall and produces 9-inch beans all summer.

Dry beans are usually bush plants and take about 100 days to mature. They include kidney, pinto and navy beans. A popular selection for home growers is the red-and-white-spotted **'Jacob's Cattle.'** A heat lover, **'Red Noodle'** produces 18-inch, stringless, red-burgundy beans. These sweet beans form clusters.

The color fades when cooked, but they're good enough to eat fresh.

Shell beans (wren's eggs, horticultural beans, bird eggs, speckled cranberries, October beans) come in both pole and dwarf varieties and can produce big harvests in small gardens. Most beans can be used as shell (or shelling) beans, which have the pods removed before they are cooked or dried. One selection that is highly coveted for shell bean use is **'Supremo,'** which is ready for harvest in 85 days.

V. faba (broad bean, fava bean)
'**Sweet Lorane**' has great flavor and
cold hardiness. It is ready for harvest
in 90–140 days. It produces fragrant
flowers followed by tough-skinned
pods. They must be soaked overnight
before using. '**Broad Windsor**' grows
4 feet tall and produces 4- to 5-inch
pods containing 5–7 beans. These
wonderfully thick broad beans are
mature in 80 days when sown in
spring, 240 days if sown in fall. Lovely
heirloom '**Crimson Flowered**' dates
back to the 18th century. It matures
in 95 days and produces crimson
flowers and upright, tasty pods. This
selection is ideal for growing in containers, borders or as an ornamental
vegetable.

Problems and Pests

Pick beans only when plants are dry
to reduce the spread of disease. Problems with leaf spot, bacterial blight,
rust, bean beetles and aphids can
occur. Disease-infected plants
should be destroyed, not composted,
once you've harvested what you can.

Beets

Beta

Beets are not only delicious but also versatile. The plump, rounded or cylindrical roots are the most commonly eaten part. The nutritious tops are also edible and compare in flavor to spinach and Swiss chard. Beets and chard are closely related. They are members of the genus *Beta*.

Starting

The corky, wrinkled seed of a beet is actually a dry fruit that contains several tiny seeds. Plant it directly in the garden around the last frost date. Even if you space seeds 3–6 inches apart, you will probably have to thin a bit because several plants can sprout from each fruit. Beets are fairly quick to mature, and a second crop can often be planted in midsummer for a fall harvest.

Growing

Beets grow well in **full sun** or **partial shade**. They grow best in cool weather. The soil should be **fertile, moist** and **well drained**. Mulch lightly with compost to maintain moisture and improve soil texture.

Harvesting

Beets mature in 45–80 days, depending on the variety. Short-season beets are best for immediate eating and preserving, and long-season beets are the better choice for storing over winter. Pick beets as soon as they are big enough to eat. They are tender when young but can become woody as they mature.

You can pick beet leaves without pulling up the entire beet if you want to use them for fresh or steamed greens. Don't pull all the leaves off a beet; just remove a few at a time from any one plant.

Roast beets are particularly delectable and please even those who say they don't like beets. Just toss them with a little olive oil and salt, cover and roast about 45 minutes, or until a knife slices easily through the largest beet.

Tips

Beets have attractive red-veined, dark green foliage. These plants look good when planted in small groups in a border, and they make interesting edging plants. For a lovely edible display, try them in large mixed containers.

Recommended

B. vulgaris forms a dense rosette of glossy, dark green leaves, often with deep red stems and veins. It grows 8–18 inches tall and spreads 4–8 inches. There are many cultivars available; here are some of the more common selections. **'Alto'** produces a very sweet, natural flavor and uniform roots. The smooth, red skin and flesh is free from rings and blemishes and often stands slightly above ground but can be covered or mounded with soil. **'Bull's Blood'** matures in 45 days as a salad leaf, and 70 days for roots. Its dark, rich foliage is commonly used as a salad green. **'Detroit Dark Red'** has dark red beets and was developed from the heirloom **'Detroit.' 'Golden Detroit'** has red skin and yellow flesh. **'Early Wonder'** and **'Red Ace'** are good red, round cultivars. **'Pablo'** is a bright red baby beet. **'Wodan'** is a bright red hybrid with a rounded shape, sweet, earthy flavor and young leaves that can be used as an alternative to spinach. This hybrid is ideal for pickling, particularly as a baby beet. **'Ruby Queen'** is an early selection, ready in 48–55 days. This smooth-skinned, buttery sweet beet is bright red with

short tops. **'Cylindra Formanova'** ('Butter Slicer') produces carrot-like roots 8 inches long and is ideal for slicing or freezing.

Novelty beet selections have been quite popular lately because of their coloration and shape, including the following. **'Albina Vereduna'** is ready for harvest in 70 days, producing crisp, white flesh with a sweet flavor surpassing most red selections. The curly and wavy leaves are beautiful and also delicious and nutritious in salads. **'Chioggia'** is an heirloom cultivar that produces red-and-white-ringed roots. **'Dolce Di Chioggia'** is ready in 55 days, producing red-and-white-striped flesh with a sweet flavor. When cut, the concentric circles of color from this heirloom variety can be used raw or cooked, as can the leaves.

'Rodina' has a red, cylindrical root. **'Touchstone Gold'** is ready for harvest is 60 days, producing bright green foliage and sweet, tender, golden roots with blushed skins and yellow flesh. This selection is one of the best for pickling.

Problems and Pests

Beets are generally problem free, but occasional trouble with scab, root maggots and flea beetles can occur.

Never fear if you get beet juice on your clothing; it won't stain. Dyers have been unsuccessfully trying to find a fixative for beet juice for centuries. Chemists inform us that the red molecule in beets is very large and doesn't adhere to other molecules, so a fixative is unlikely to ever be found.

Broccoli

Brassica

Although usually thought of as a vegetable, broccoli could more accurately be called an edible flower. The large, dense flower clusters are generally eaten, though the stems and leaves are also edible, not to mention jam-packed with minerals, vitamins and micronutrients. Broccoli is a member of the cabbage family.

Starting

Broccoli can be started from seed indoors or planted directly into the garden. Sow seeds indoors 4–6 weeks before the last frost date. Seedlings can withstand limited cold, so get a jumpstart on the season and plant outside 2–4 weeks before the last frost date. In warm areas, set out plants in late summer, fall or winter.

Until about 60 years ago, broccoli had an identity problem. It was lumped together with cauliflower, its cousin.

Growing

Broccoli grows best in **full sun**. The soil should be **fertile, moist** and **well drained**. Broccoli performs best in cooler weather, when nights are 60–70° F and days reach 80° F. Hot weather turns broccoli bitter and may cause bolting. Mix compost into the soil, and add a layer of mulch to keep the soil moist. Don't let this plant dry out excessively or it will delay flowering.

Harvesting

Broccoli forms a central head (broccoli), and some varieties (known as sprouting broccoli) also produce side shoots. Pick the heads by cutting them cleanly from the plant with a sharp knife. If you leave them too long on the plant, the bright yellow flowers will open.

Choosing a side-shoot-producing plant versus a main-head-only variety is a matter of personal preference. If you have a large family or plan to freeze some florets, you may prefer a large-headed selection. If there are only a few people in the household, or you want to enjoy the broccoli for longer without storing any, you may prefer the small-headed varieties that produce plenty of side shoots.

Tips

Broccoli, with its blue-green foliage, is an interesting accent plant. Tuck it in groups of three in your borders for contrast. This plant is subject to many pests and diseases. Plant it in small groups rather than rows to lessen the severity of potential problems.

Recommended

B. oleracea var. *botrytis* is an upright plant with a stout, leafy central stem. Flowers form at the top of the plant and sometimes on side shoots that emerge from just above each leaf. Plants grow 12–36 inches tall and spread 12–18 inches. Maturity dates vary from 45 to 100 days. '**Green Goliath**' sends out lots of

'Broccoli Romanesco'

side shoots during an extended 3 week harvest rather than all at once. Popular in many areas of California, **'Marathon'** produces in 97 days. **'Piracicaba'** has a looser head and many side shoots; it can handle warmer weather. **'Belstar'** produces well-domed, small-beaded, deep green heads. Slow-bolting heirloom **'Calbrese'** ('Calabria') produces plenty of side shoots. Sprouting Italian heirloom **'De Cicco'** has edible leaves and produces many side shoots. Mildew-resistant **'Gypsy'** produces a large central head and is one of the most heat-tolerant cultivars. **'Nutri-Bud'** is an early-maturing variety; look for lots of side shoots after the main head is cut. **'Packman'** is an earlier selection, ready in 55 days. It bears large, domed heads with medium-sized beads. One of the most prolific side shoot producers, it tolerates hot weather and can be planted in succession. **'Premium Crop'** is an All-America Selections winner that is early to mature and produces plenty of side shoots.

Broccoli is also available in novelty selections. **'Apollo'** (broccoli crossed with asparagus) is ready in 60–90 days. Harvest the main floret early and leave plenty of room for the tender, sweet, delicious side shoots. This broccoli cross is often found at specialty groceries. Beautiful light green heirloom **'Broccoli Romanesco'** features unusual spires and swirls and dates back to the 16th century. Another heirloom, **'Purple Sprouting,'** has unusual dark purple sprouts. A long-season grower, it requires 120 (summer) to 200 (winter) days till harvest.

B. rapa ruvo (raab, broccoletto) is a delicious, quick-sprouting form of broccoli. **'Cima de Rapa'** produces spicy, edible leaves, shoots and flower buds—what some might call mini broccoli. **'Spring Raab'** is ready in 42 days, with large, slow-to-bolt plants. This selection is considered one of the best for successive plantings for continuous harvests, and it's great in stir-fries.

Problems and Pests

Problems with cutworms, leaf miners, caterpillars, root maggots, cabbage white butterflies, white rust, downy mildew and powdery mildew can occur. Avoid planting any Brassica in the same spot in successive years.

Cabbage white butterflies are common pests for all members of the Brassica family, and their tiny green caterpillar larvae can be tough to spot in a head of broccoli. Break heads into pieces and soak them in salted water for 10 or so minutes before cooking. Doing so kills the larvae and causes them to float to the surface.

Brussels Sprouts

Brassica

Love them or hate them, Brussels sprouts are at the very least a garden curiosity. The sprouts form on the stout central stem at the base of each leaf. Looking like mini-cabbages, the display is unique and eye-catching.

Starting

Buy small transplants or start seeds indoors about 6 weeks before you expect to put them in the ground. Sowing seeds into peat pots or pellets makes transplanting easy. Cold-region gardeners should plant in spring for fall harvest. In warm areas, plant in late summer or fall for spring harvest.

Growing

Brussels sprouts grow well in **full sun**. The soil should be **fertile, moist** and **well drained**. Brussels sprouts need a long growing season to produce sprouts of any appreciable size, so they should be planted out as early as possible. Plan on dedicating part of your garden to them for an extended period. Regular moisture encourages them to mature quickly, so keep the soil well mulched. Once you see sprouts starting to form, you may wish to remove some of the top stem leaves to give the sprouts more room to grow.

Nutrient rich and fiber packed, Brussels sprouts deserve a more prominent place on our plates. People who complain that sprouts are mushy or bitter have probably had ones that were poorly prepared. When picked after a light frost, steamed so that they are cooked just through to the center and served with butter, they are delicious. You can also roast them in the oven to bring out their sweetness.

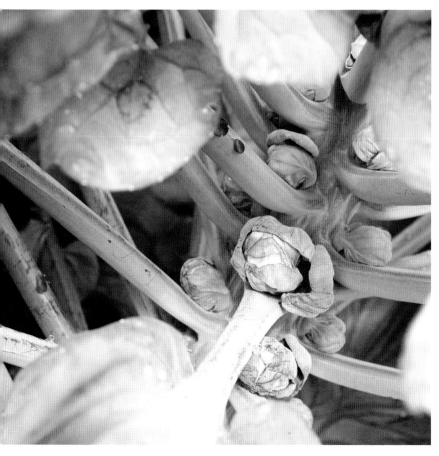

Harvesting

Pick sprouts as soon as they are large and plump, but before they begin to open. A light frost can improve their flavor. The entire plant can be pulled up, and if you remove the roots, leaves and top of the plant, the sprouts can be stored on the stem in a cool place for up to 4 weeks. Be sure to keep an eye on them because they can go bad quickly. They can also be frozen for later use.

Tips

Brussels sprouts create a leafy backdrop for flowering annuals and perennials;

then, just as the garden is fading, they create an interesting focal point as the plump little sprouts develop.

Recommended

B. oleracea var. *gemnifera* is an upright plant that develops a single leafy stem. Sprouts form at the base of each leaf along the stem. The leaves are blue-green, often with white midribs and stems. Available in early-, mid- and late-season varieties, some Brussels sprouts offer ongoing harvest over several weeks. **'Oliver,'** an early-season choice, provides sprouts in 90 days.

Other popular cultivars include **'Bubbles,'** **'Long Island Improved'** and **'Tasty Nuggets.'** Try mid-season **'United'** along the coast. For something unusual, try **'Rubine,'** a purple-red heirloom.

Problems and Pests

Problems with cutworms, leaf miners, caterpillars, root maggots, aphids, cabbage white butterfly larvae, white rust, downy mildew and powdery mildew can occur.

To avoid overcooking Brussels sprouts, cut an X about one-quarter of the way through each sprout to help the inside cook at the same rate as the outside.

Cabbage & Oriental Cabbage

Brassica

Cabbages of every size, shape and texture are easy to grow, and they create a dense, leafy, often colorful display. You'll find them in green with smooth leaves, green with very crinkled leaves and red or purple, usually with smooth leaves. Oriental cabbage includes a diverse collection of Asian vegetables such as bok choi, tatsoi and napa cabbage.

Starting

Start seeds indoors about 4–6 weeks before you plan to transplant the seedlings outdoors. You can also direct sow cabbage into the garden around the last frost date as long as the soil has warmed up a bit. Where winters are mild, plant in fall or winter. If you find average cabbages too large, plant them closer together to get smaller, tighter heads.

Once a specialty item, Oriental cabbage (bok choi, pak choi) plants can now be found in many nurseries.

Growing

Cabbages grow best in **full sun** but will grow in partial shade in hot areas. They prefer cool growing conditions and benefit from mulch to retain moisture during hot weather. The soil should be **fertile, moist** and **well drained**.

Oriental cabbage likes the same conditions but is more tolerant of warm, humid weather than some of the other members of the Brassica family. These Asian greens flourish in winter gardens in the southern part of the state and along the coast. In many parts of California, they can be grown year-round, though they may bolt in hot summers.

Harvesting

The leaves of young cabbage plants can be eaten. When a good-sized head has

'Early Jersey Wakefield'

Savoy cabbage (above); Oriental cabbage (below)

developed, cut it cleanly from the plant. Smaller heads often develop once the main head has been cut. Cabbages that take a long time to mature (3–4 months from transplant) generally store better than types that mature quickly (7–8 weeks from transplant).

Oriental cabbage comes in two basic forms: solid heads that are cut whole, and looser heads with leaves that can be removed as needed.

Tips

Grow several varieties of cabbages because the different colors, textures and maturing times create a more interesting display in rows or in mixed borders.

Oriental cabbage can be grown in containers and combined with other edible or flowering plants.

Recommended

B. oleracea var. *capitata* (cabbage) is a low, leafy rosette that develops a dense head during summer and fall. Leaves may be green, blue-green, red or purple and smooth or crinkled. It matures in 60–140 days, depending on the variety.

Some popular smooth-leaved, green varieties are **'Copenhagen Market,'** **'Famosa,'** **'Golden Acre,'** **'Point One'** and **'Tendersweet.'** Heirloom **'Early Jersey Wakefield'** dates to the mid-1800s and has a compact size that makes it perfect for smaller gardens. Mid- to late-season varieties include **'Greenback,'** **'Late Flat Dutch'** and **'Savor.'**

Smooth-leaved green varieties (above and below)

Popular crinkled or savoy types include '**Savoy Ace**' and '**Savoy King**.'

Popular red cabbages include '**Cabbage Salad Delight**,' '**Ruby Perfection**,' '**Ruby Ball Hybrid**' and '**Red Head**.'

B. rapa subsp. *chinensis* (pac choi, bok choi) forms a loose clump of blue-green leaves with thick, fleshy, white or light green stems. There are three types: green stem, white stem and specialty. '**Hanakan**' is a compact Japanese green stem hybrid that is ready to harvest in 45 days. '**Dwarf Pak Choi**' (baby bok choi) is a white-stemmed variety. It is mild in flavor, with white stems and ribs and deep green leaves. Harvest when it is 4 inches tall. '**Golden Yellow**' is a specialty heat-tolerant hybrid that bears yellowish green leaves from root to tip. The texture is softer than other varieties but the flavor is the same. **'Red Violet Tatsoi'** is a deep purple variety with a mild mustard flavor.

B. rapa* subsp. *pekinensis (Chinese cabbage, napa cabbage) forms a dense head of tightly packed leaves. There are four types: barrel head, loose head, fluffy top and Michihili. **'Optiko'** has a barrel shape and prominent white veins and ribs. It can be used like a savoy cabbage. It matures faster than most others and is mild tasting with a crisp texture. **'Kaisin Hakusai'** is a fluffy top cabbage with frilly outer leaves that become more blanched toward the center. **'Green Rocket,'** a Michihili type, resembles an endive or chicory head, but in jumbo size. This Chinese cabbage is grown for its sweetness. The tight heads are more mild and tender than western cabbages.

Problems and Pests

Problems with cutworms, leaf miners, caterpillars, root maggots, aphids, cabbage white butterfly larvae, white rust, downy mildew and powdery mildew can occur.

All members of the Brassica family are susceptible to many of the same pests and diseases. Don't plant them in the same spot 2 years in a row, particularly if you've had disease problems in that area.

An interesting addition to the garden, Oriental cabbage is also a tasty ingredient in stir-fries and soups.

To protect cabbage from egg-laying moths, create a plastic butterfly screen. Simply hammer one stake into the ground at each corner of the row or patch of cabbage. Cut out simple, quarter-sized shapes of moths or butterflies from a white plastic container, such as an ice cream pail lid or sour cream container, and thread them onto fishing line. Attach the ends of the line to the stakes, creating a grid pattern. A little goes a long way to show the cabbage butterflies that this territory has already been taken and is off limits.

A mix of Oriental cabbage varieties and bok choi

Carrots

Daucus

With an array of bright colors, crunchy carrots are one of those "Wow!" vegetables beloved by both adults and children. Once upon a time, you needed a deep bed to accommodate the long roots. New hybrids and more readily available heirlooms assure that there's a carrot for every garden.

Starting

Carrots can be sown directly into the garden once the last frost date has passed and the soil has warmed up. The seeds are very tiny and can be difficult to plant evenly. Mix them with sand before sowing for more even distribution, or look for coated, pelleted seeds for easy handling. Cover seeds very lightly with sand or compost because they can't sprout through too much soil. Keep the seedbed moist to encourage even germination.

Growing

Carrots grow best in **full sun**. The soil should be **average to fertile, well drained** and **deeply prepared**. Carrots are a root vegetable, and many varieties require soil to be loose and free of rocks to a depth of 8–12 inches. This gives them plenty of space to develop and makes them easier to pull when ready. In rocky or shallow soil, consider planting carrots in raised beds to provide deeper, looser soil; or just grow shorter varieties. Tiny carrots with shallower roots are also available.

Spacing carrots is a gradual process. As they develop, pull a few out to leave room for others to fill in. This thinning process indicates how well they are developing and when they will be ready to harvest. The root can be eaten at all stages of development.

Harvesting

Never judge carrots by their greens. Big, bushy tops are no indication that carrots are ready for picking.

Many supermarket varieties sold as "baby" carrots are whittled-to-size adults. By growing your own, you'll get to enjoy the flavor of real young carrots.

As the roots grow, you will often see carrot tops at or just above soil level—a better indication of development. In loose soil, you can pull them with a good grip on the greens. Heavier soil may demand a garden fork to dig them up without breakage.

To keep carrots for a long time, store them in a cold, frost-free place in containers of moistened sand.

Tips

Carrots make an excellent ornamental grouping or edging plant. The feathery foliage provides an attractive background for flowers and plants with ornamental foliage. Carrots can also be grown in containers with adequate depth for root growth.

Recommended

D. carota var. sativus forms a bushy mound of feathery foliage. It matures in 50–75 days. The edible roots may be orange, red, yellow, white or purple. They come in a variety of shapes, from long and slender to short and round.

Some of the more standard selections include the following. **'Baby Babette'** produces baby carrots. **'Napoli'** is an early-maturing, sweet carrot. **'Mignon'** is ready for harvest in 70 days, producing rich, tender,

'Cosmic Purple' (above); 'Mini Sweet' (below)

orange roots bred for growing as baby carrots. Because of this trait, 'Mignon' is ideal for successive sowings throughout the growing season. **'Danvers'** offers 6- to 7-inch-long roots with firm flesh, an excellent sweet flavor and strong tops, which make for easy pulling. **'Ithaca'** is a reliable grower that produces 7-inch-long carrots in less-than-perfect conditions. **'Fly Away'** was bred to be unattractive to flies, and is very sweet and adaptable to tough environmental conditions. **'Resistafly'** is rust fly resistant. **'Royal Chantenay'** is an heirloom carrot with a deep orange core. **'Scarlet Nantes'** ('Nantes'), one of the most popular carrots, is a sweet heirloom carrot. **'Sweetness'** is an extra-early Nantes carrot, ready in 55 days bearing heavy yields of

8-inch-long carrots. Japanese '**Mini Sweet**' is a tender, orange-red variety that is ready in 60 days. Small and slim, averaging 4 inches in length, this carrot is great raw, straight out of the soil.

There are many novelty selections based on color, shape and other attributes. '**Atomic Red**' is tapered, bright red and measures up to 8 inches long. This crispy carrot tastes great regardless of size and intensifies in color when cooked. '**Cosmic Purple**' has smooth, purple skin and coreless, orange flesh. The 7-inch-long roots have a sweet flavor, but the color fades after cooking, so enjoy this selection raw in a salad. '**Nutri Red**' is a purple-red carrot high in lycopene, a precursor to beta-carotene. '**Purple Haze**' is a dark (almost black) purple-skinned,

orange-fleshed carrot. '**White Satin**' is a white Nantes carrot with exceptionally sweet flesh. It has an excellent yield, is ready in 72 days and can grow up to 8 inches long. '**Rainbow Mix**' is often found in seed catalogs, offering a variety of carrot selections in different colors, maturity periods, flavors and sizes, but all are in shades of peach, orange, yellow, white and purple.

Problems and Pests

Carrot rust flies and root maggots can sometimes be troublesome.

Carrots weren't originally orange; they were either purple or a faded version of the orange we now know. Artwork painted over 200 years ago depicts carrots in pale yellows, dark purples and reds.

Cauliflower

Brassica

If you think of pure white heads when you think of cauliflower, you may be surprised by all the different colors available through seed vendors. Orange, purple and green are all great possibilities. Tuck a few plants here and there in your mixed borders to shake things up a bit and increase your harvest.

Starting

Cauliflower can be sown directly into the garden around the last frost date, or you can start it indoors about 4 weeks before you plan to set it outdoors. In areas where winters are mild, plant in fall or winter.

Growing

Cauliflower grows best in **full sun**. The soil should be **fertile, moist** and **well drained**. This plant favors cool, humid weather. In warm areas, search out heat-resistant varieties

The word cauliflower means "flowered cabbage."

and avoid planting for summer harvest. Cauliflower must have rich soil that stays evenly moist, or heads may form poorly, if at all. Mix plenty of compost into the soil, and mulch with compost to help keep the soil moist.

Harvesting

Unlike broccoli, most cauliflower does not develop secondary heads once the main one is cut. Cut the head cleanly from the plant when it is mature. You can then compost the plant.

Tips

White cauliflower may turn yellow or greenish unless it is protected from the sun. To preserve the white color, tie some of the outer leaves together over

the head with elastic or string when you first notice the head forming.

Unlike white cauliflower, the purple-, green-, yellow- or orange-headed varieties need no shading while they develop. The colored selections are pretty when planted into mixed ornamental gardens.

Recommended

B. oleracea var. *botrytis* is leafy and upright with dense, edible flower clusters in the center of the plant. Most selections take 70–85 days to mature, though some mature in as few as 45 days.

Popular white-headed cultivars include 'Snowball,' 'Symphony' and the heat-tolerant 'Snow King.' 'Early Snowball' takes 50 days from sowing to produce bright white heads with deep curds. This large selection is also great for freezing. 'Snow Crown' is ready in 53 days and is considered to be one of the easiest selections to grow due to its vigor and tough constitution. It produces medium-sized, domed heads up to 8 inches across.

'Graffiti' and 'Violet Queen' are purple-headed cultivars. 'Graffiti' is the later selection, bearing dark

purple heads in 80 days. Unlike 'Violet Queen,' it produces more of a "true" cauliflower head, rather than a cluster of tinier heads, on very large plants. **'Violetta di Sicilia'** is an Italian heirloom that produces side shoots after the main head is cut.

Green-headed cultivars include **'Green Harmony'** and heat-tolerant **'Veronica,'** whose florets form pointed, tapering peaks. **'Romanesco White Gold'** has a space-age appearance, producing spirally, lime green florets with a broccoli flavor and cauliflower texture. **'Broccoverde'** is another green-headed cauliflower. It has medium-sized, domed heads. This selection is very sweet and tolerates warmer zones.

'Cheddar' is a popular orange-headed cultivar that contains 25 times the amount of vitamin A as white cauliflower. **'Orange Bouquet'** is ready in 60 days, producing pale orange heads also high in vitamin A. If you simply can't decide, try **'Multicolor Blend,'** with orange, purple and green heads.

Problems and Pests

Problems with cutworms, leaf miners, caterpillars, root maggots, aphids, cabbage white butterfly larvae, white rust, downy mildew and powdery mildew can occur. Like its family member broccoli, cauliflower attracts green caterpillar larvae. Break heads into pieces and soak them in salted water for 10 minutes or so before cooking. This kills the larvae and causes them to float to the surface.

Purple cauliflower generally turns green when cooked.

Celery & Celeriac

Apium

Tender, ribbed stalks of fresh garden celery are quite different from those we get at the store. The flavor of unblanched stems is much stronger, for example, and some people like them better. Celeriac, also known as celery root, is used raw in salads or cooked in soups and stews.

Starting

Celery and celeriac thrive in warmth but not heat. In cool regions, start seed indoors at least 8–12 weeks before planting outside. Be patient; seed can take up to 3 weeks to germinate. Be sure to keep the planting medium moist, but not soggy. Plant out once the last frost date has passed and the soil has warmed up. In warm areas, set plants out in fall.

Celery and celeriac seeds are tiny; look for coated, pelleted varieties for easy handling. Celery is also available in nursery packs. Celeriac is less commonly grown and best purchased as seed.

Growing

Celery and celeriac grow best in **full sun** but enjoy light or afternoon shade in hot weather. The soil should be **fertile, humus rich, moist** and **well drained**. Allowing soil to dry out too much yields poor quality, bad-tasting vegetables. Mulch plants to conserve moisture.

Celeriac (below)

Blanching is a gardening technique usually used on bitter-tasting vegetables. Partially or completely depriving the plant of light sweetens the flavor. Though many devices have been developed to make blanching easier, a good mound of soil or mulch will do the job.

In late summer, you can mound soil around the celery stalks, wrap them in newspaper or surround the base of each plant with a milk carton with the top and bottom cut out to provide shade. This encourages the familiar pale green stems. Unblanched stalks have a stronger flavor that some people prefer. Celeriac needs no blanching.

Harvesting

Celery stalks can be harvested 1–2 at a time from each plant for most of summer. If you are blanching the stems before picking, they will be ready for harvest 2–3 weeks after the stalks are covered. A light touch of frost can sweeten the flavor.

Celeriac should be harvested before the first fall frost. Pull plants up, remove the leaves and store the knobby roots the same way you would beets or carrots, in a cold, frost-free location in a container of moistened sand.

Tips

Celery and celeriac have light green leaves that create a very bushy back-drop for flowering plants with less attractive, spindly growth.

Recommended

A. graveolens var. *dulce* (celery) is a bushy, upright plant with attrac-tive, light to bright green foliage. It matures in 100–120 days. **'Giant Pascal,' 'Golden Self-Blanching'** and **'Tall Utah 52-70'** are popular cultivars. The heirloom **'Red Stalk'** stays red when cooked. **'Tango'** is ready in 80 days, producing

strong flavor. The stalks are tender, with less fiber, and the plant tolerates excessive heat and moisture stress better than most varieties.

A. graveolens **var.** *secalinum* **'Affina'** (cutting celery) is grown more for the greens than anything else. The stalks don't develop like other cultivars do, so this selection is considered to be an immature form of celery. The plants are ready for harvest in 120 days, if not sooner, producing a clump of slender stems and bright green leaves for cutting. Harvest and use the leaves readily to promote further, denser growth throughout the growing season.

A. graveolens **var.** *rapaceum* (celeriac) forms a bushy, bright green plant that develops a thick, knobby, bulbous root. It matures in 100–120 days. **'Brilliant,' 'Mentor,' 'Ibis,' 'Diamant'** and **'Giant Prague'** are popular cultivars.

Problems and Pests

Problems with fungal blight, mosaic virus, *Fusarium* wilt, bacterial and fungal rot, leaf spot and caterpillars can occur.

Cold nights can cause celery to flower, leaving the stalks inedible, or at least unpalatable.

Chard

Beta

A type of beet, chard is one of the garden's most useful vegetables. The wide range of colors makes it a valuable ornamental addition to beds, borders and even container gardens. Mild areas can grow it year-round.

Starting

The corky, wrinkled seed of chard is actually a dry fruit that contains several tiny seeds. Plant the dry fruit directly in the garden around the last frost date. Where winters are mild, plant in spring or fall. You will probably have to thin the plants a bit even if you space the seeds 3–6 inches apart because several plants can sprout from each fruit. Nursery plants are easy to find.

Growing

Chard grows well in **full sun** or **partial shade**. It grows best in cool weather. The soil should be **fertile, moist** and **well drained**. Mulch lightly with compost to maintain moisture and improve soil texture.

Harvesting

Chard matures quickly, and a few leaves can be plucked from each plant every week or so. You can generally start picking leaves about 1 month after the seed sprouts.

Tips

Chard has very decorative foliage. Although the leaves are usually glossy green, the stems and veins are often brightly colored in shades of red, pink, white, yellow or orange. When planted in small groups in your borders, chard adds a colorful touch. The bushy, clumping habit also makes it well suited to mixed container plantings.

Recommended

B. vulgaris* subsp. *cicla forms a clump of green, purple, red or bronze, glossy leaves that are often deeply crinkled or savoyed. Stems and veins may be pale green, white, yellow, orange, pink, red or purple. Plants grow 8–18 inches tall and spread about 12 inches. Popular cultivars include **'Bright Lights,'** an All-America Selections winner that produces a mix of red, white, pink, green, orange, gold, violet and yellow stems, mostly solid but occasionally striped, with green or bronze foliage; **'Fordhook Giant,'** a white-stemmed heirloom; **'Gazelle,'** which produces dark green leaves that contrast with red stems and veins, all in 58 days; **'Lucullus,'** with light green, incredibly crumpled, curly leaves and broad stems with rounded, white ribs; sweet, mild **'Neon Glow,'** with gold and magenta stems; **'Orange Fantasia,'** with orange stems; **'Perpetual,'** a heat-resistant, non-bolting cultivar with small, pale green stems and spinach-like leaves; **'Rainbow,'** with a combination of red, orange, yellow or white stems; **'Scarlet Charlotte,'** with bright red stems; and **'Silverado,'** with creamy white stems.

Problems and Pests

Rare problems with downy mildew, powdery mildew, leaf miners, aphids, caterpillars and root rot can occur.

Try chard instead of spinach in recipes. It's less temperamental in the garden and has a similar flavor and texture.

'Bright Lights'

Corn

Zea

Corn is believed to have originated in South America. Widely grown by native peoples in both North and South America, corn is one of the "three sisters" of native gardens: corn, beans and squash. All three were grown together as companions. The beans fixed nitrogen in the soil and could climb up the corn for support. The large leaves of squash shaded the soil and kept weeds to a minimum.

Starting

Start seed directly in the garden
2 weeks after the last frost date; seed
will rot if the soil is too cool. Depending on the variety you choose, corn
can take from 75 to 110 days to
mature. If your growing season is
short or the soil is slow to warm,
you may prefer to start your corn
4–6 weeks early in peat pots and
transplant it to the garden after
the last frost date.

*There are ornamental varieties of corn
available: some, such as 'Fiesta' and
'Seneca Indian,' have colorful kernels;
others, such as 'Harlequin' and
'Variegata,' have foliage striped in
red, green and white or creamy white,
respectively.*

Growing

Corn grows best in **full sun**. The soil should be **fertile, moist** and **well drained**. Water deeply. As the plant develops, you can mound more soil around its base; the stem will develop roots in this soil, and the plant will be stronger and less likely to blow over in a strong wind. Look for early-, mid- and late-season varieties to keep corn on your table all season long.

Resist the temptation to remove the tassels at the top of the plant. As the male part of the plant, tassels supply pollen, which falls onto the

silk, the female portion of the plant. Each silk thread is attached to a kernel. If no pollen falls onto the silk, no kernel will form. Shaking plants when pollen is being shed can increase pollination.

Harvesting

Corn is ready to pick when the silks start to turn brown and the kernels are plump. Check for readiness by popping a kernel. Watery liquid means you're too early, and no liquid means you're too late. If you get milky liquid, pick the corn and enjoy it.

Use heirloom varieties as quickly as possible after picking because they begin to turn starchy as soon as they are picked. Some newer varieties have been genetically modified to increase sweetness. These can be stored for a while with no loss of sweetness.

Tips

Corn is an architectural grass that looks similar to some of the upright ornamental grasses, such as miscanthus. Plant it in groups of 5–9 in your beds and borders. Also, because corn is wind pollinated, plants need to be fairly close together for pollination to occur. Planting in groups rather than rows improves pollination rates when growing only a few plants.

To ensure maximum sweetness, cobs should be immersed in ice cold water as soon as possible after picking, and left in the water until cooked. Keep the cobs out of the hot sun as much as possible. These two steps are vital because the sugars in the kernels quickly convert to starches after the cobs are harvested, producing a less sweet product.

Corn is an ingredient in more than 3000 grocery products.

Recommended

Z. mays is a sturdy, upright grass with bright green leaves with undulating edges. Plants grow 4–8 feet tall and spread 12–24 inches. **Var. *rugosa*** (sweet corn) matures in 65–80 days and falls into several sweetness categories that gauge both degree of sweetness and how quickly sugar turns to starch once the corn is picked. Kernels can be white or yellow, or a combination. For fun, **var. *praecox*** (popcorn) matures in 100–110 days and has shorter cobs with hard, yellow, white or red kernels.

Mirai Series is a group of hybrids regarded as one of the most delicious corn series available.

'**Mirai Yellow**' is ready in 75 days, bearing succulent cobs 7–8 inches long with super tender, sweet corn. '**Mirai Bicolor**' produces cobs up to 8½ inches long with golden yellow, tender, sweet kernels, with the occasional white kernel thrown in. '**Mirai White**' is an albino form, bearing extra-tender, sweet, white cobs with kernels to the tip.

Sugar-enhanced selections are also very popular and include mid-season '**Bodacious**,' white '**How Sweet It Is**' and yellow '**Kandy Korn**' and '**Breeder's Choice**.'

Super sweet selections include yellow '**Early Extra Sweet**,' bicolor '**Ivory 'n' Gold**' and '**Butterfruit**,' and yellow '**Sweetie**' and '**Illini Gold**.'

If you prefer heirloom varieties that have not been genetically modified, try '**Golden Bantam**,' with sweet, yellow, 6- to 7-inch ears, and '**Stowell's Evergreen**,' a white sweet corn introduced in 1848.

Problems and Pests

Corn earworms, aphids, caterpillars, downy mildew, rust, smut and fungal leaf spots can cause problems for corn.

Avoid growing both popcorn and sweet corn, or keep them well separated. They can cross-pollinate, which can make both of them inedible.

Cucumbers

Cucumis

Whether you have a passion for pickling or think a salad just isn't a salad without the cool crispness of cukes, you have a wide range to choose from in the California garden. And there's no doubt about it—homegrown cucumbers are far superior to anything you can buy at your local grocer.

Starting

Cucumbers can be started indoors about 4 weeks before the last frost date or can be sown directly into the garden once the last frost date has passed and the soil has warmed up. If you start them inside, use peat pots to avoid damaging the roots.

Growing

Cucumbers grow well in **full sun**. The soil should be **fertile, moist** and **well drained**. Consistent moisture is important during germination and fruit production. If you're short on space, grow them up a trellis or other support by tying vines with strips of old nylons or other soft ties to avoid damaging the plants.

New varieties have more female flowers, and these produce earlier with better yields.

Harvesting

Harvest timing depends on cucumber type. Pick pickling cucumbers when they are young and small. Harvest slicing cucumbers when small if you want to pickle them; let them mature for other uses. Pick long, slender Oriental cucumbers when mature.

Tips

Cucumbers are versatile trailing plants. They can be left to wind their way through the other plants in your garden or grown up trellises or other supports. The mound-forming varieties make attractive additions to container gardens.

Recommended

C. sativus is a trailing annual vine with coarse leaves and bristly stems. It matures in 45–60 days. Popular

'Lemon' (above)

Cucumbers keep producing as long as the fruit doesn't stay on the vines too long. Pick cucumbers as soon as they are a good size for eating. The more you pick, the more they will produce.

slicing and salad cucumbers include the long, slender **'English Telegraph'** and **'Sweet Success'**; All-America Selections winner **'Fanfare,'** a prolific bush selection; and the high-yielding **'Stonewall.'** **'Armenian'** is an heirloom cucumber. This strong, vigorous grower is ready in 50–55 days, producing fruit with thin, light green skin resembling Asian varieties. **'Burpless'** is another slicing cucumber, ready in 62 days. It was bred for those who experience gassiness after eating cucumbers. This hybrid is mild and non-astringent, with a thin, tender skin—no peeling required, and no gas. Heirloom **'Straight Eight'** is ready in 60 days and is said to have superb flavor compared to other selections. It produces mid-green, uniformly shaped, 8-inch-long cucumbers. For containers, try disease-resistant dwarf **'Bush Slicer'** and high-yielding, space-saving **'Spacemaster.'**

Two highly recommended novelty cucumbers are **'Tondo di Manduria'** and **'Lemon.'** The first, native to Italy, is ready in 60–70 days and produces rounded fruits about the size of a lemon, lightly striped with dark and light green. If left to grow larger, the fruit can be treated similar to a melon. With low sugar levels, this cucumber is ideal for a diabetic diet. The second of the two is an heirloom variety, bearing 3- to 4-inch oval, bright yellow fruits on vigorous vines. This prolific cucumber has a slight lemon flavor and fragrance in late stages of development. **'Beit Alpha'** is a Lebanese type originating from the Middle East. It bears 8- to 10-inch smooth, medium green

fruit with thin skin. It is highly disease resistant and is ready in 55 days. Another popular baby Persian variety, disease-resistant **'Green Fingers,'** has 3- to 5-inch fruit. **'Long White'** is ready in 85 days. This cucumber is not bitter and has a thin, tender, white skin. It has firm flesh with a sweet but tangy flavor.

Pickling cucumbers are harvested when small, and popular cultivars include the disease-tolerant,

semi-bush **'Cross Country'** and the prolific, bushy **'Pickalot.'** Other popular varieties include **'Liberty Hybrid'** and **'Saladin.'** Want to grow pickles in containers? Try **'Pickle Bush'** and **'Pot Luck.'**

Problems and Pests

Problems with powdery mildew, downy mildew, mosaic virus, white flies, aphids, cucumber beetles, bacterial wilt, leaf spot, scab and ring spot can occur.

Eggplant
Solanum

A native of India, eggplant is a lovely, productive member of the nightshade family, which also includes tomatoes. Despite its heritage, standard eggplant—the large, heavy purple globe found in the grocery store—is known as Italian eggplant. A newcomer to many California gardens, long, slender Asian eggplant is gaining in popularity. Both types grow beautifully in summer heat.

Starting

Buy container plants or start from seed indoors 6–8 weeks before setting plants out. Place plants in the garden after any danger of frost has passed.

Growing

Eggplant grows best in **full sun** with consistent warmth (daytime temperatures between 70° F and 85° F) over a 2–3 month period. Eggplant does best in **fertile, loamy, moist, well-drained** soil. Water deeply and regularly, and mulch.

Harvesting

Harvest eggplant when it is bright, shiny and firm. Otherwise, it will turn bitter. Pick Italian eggplant when it is 4–6 inches in diameter and 6–9 inches long; harvest Asian varieties at 4–6 inches long. Cut eggplant from its woody stock with a sharp knife or scissors to avoid damaging the plant. Continuous harvesting increases production.

Tips

Eggplant develops fruit in a variety of sizes, shapes and colors. Plant several types for an interesting display. Plants are bushy and bear pretty flowers, making a welcome addition to beds and borders.

Where long, hot summers aren't the norm, consider growing eggplant near a sunny wall where it can bask in reflected heat, or put it in a movable container to catch the sun's rays wherever they land.

Recommended

S. melongena **var.** *esculentum* is a bushy, heat-loving perennial grown as an annual with small, purple or white flowers. Fruit ranges in shape from small and round to long and slender and in color from deep purple to white, with mottled variations in between. Flavor varies significantly from cultivar to cultivar; experiment to see which ones grow best and which ones you enjoy the most.

Standard, or Italian, varieties with large, purple fruit include 'Black Beauty,' 'Early Bird' and 'Dusky.' The beautiful heirloom 'Rosa Bianca' bears fruit with white and pink skin and white flesh on 24-inch-tall plants. Fruit is 5–7 inches long and 4–6 inches wide. 'Fairy Tale' is an All-America Selections winner with long, light purple, white-streaked fruit.

Asian types include 'Ichiban,' an easy-to-grow choice with 4- to 6-inch, slender, dark purple fruit, and the lovely lavender 'Asian Bride,' with 8-inch fruit and white flesh. 'Gretel' is an All-America Selections winner and produces shiny, 3- to 4-inch fruit on compact plants. 'Kermit' is a green and white Thai variety. Its compact form is well branched, supporting sets of rounded fruits 2 inches across. Extra-early 'Indian Baby' yields tiny, 1-ounce eggplants in only 40 days and keeps on producing during the season. Taiwanese heirloom 'Ping Tung Long' is heat, cold and disease resistant and features long, thin, 10- to 14-inch eggplants.

Other interesting varieties include 'Apple Green,' a mild, oval variety with 5- to 6-inch fruit. It does well even in cool, wet conditions. For a small garden or container, pretty lavender-striped **'Calliope'** is a nice choice. Harvest fruit at 2–4 inches. Lovely, easy-to-grow **'White Angel'** develops unusual white fruit 10–12 inches long, perfect for stuffing and stir-fries.

Problems and Pests

Eggplant occasionally suffers from *Fusarium* wilt. Control aphids to prevent other insect problems.

Eggplant was slow to catch on in the West after being discovered in Asia, possibly because of its nickname "mad apple" and its reputation for causing insanity.

Fennel

Foeniculum

Fennel has been part of history for thousands of years. Herbalists tout its healing capabilities; cooks use it as both vegetable and herb. All parts of fennel are edible and have a distinctive licorice-like fragrance and flavor. Florence fennel produces a large, swollen base that is eaten raw, cooked or roasted. Fennel bulbs combine well with many other vegetables in savory recipes and make an inter-esting addition to sweet recipes, too. Try adding some to your next fruit salad.

Starting

Start seeds directly in the garden after the danger of frost has passed.

Growing

Fennel grows best in **full sun**. The soil should be **average to fertile, moist** and **well drained**. Avoid planting fennel near dill or coriander because cross-pollination reduces seed production and makes the seed flavor of each one less distinct. Fennel easily self-sows.

Harvesting

Harvest fennel leaves as needed for fresh use. When seeds are ripe, in late summer or fall, harvest them by shaking the seed heads over a sheet. Dry the seeds before storing.

Florence fennel deteriorates quickly after harvest, so be sure to use it as soon as possible. Store in the refrigerator for no more than a few days.

Harvest Florence fennel as soon as the bulbous base becomes swollen. Pull plants up as needed, and harvest any left in the ground at the end of the season before the first fall frost.

Tips

Fennel is an attractive addition to a mixed bed or border. The flowers attract pollinators and predatory insects to the garden.

Recommended

F. vulgare is a short-lived perennial that forms clumps of loose, feathery foliage. It grows 24–36 inches tall and spreads 12–24 inches. Clusters of small, yellow flowers are borne in late summer. The seeds ripen in fall. The species is primarily grown for its seeds and leaves. **Var.** *azoricum* (Florence fennel, finocchio) is a biennial that forms a large, edible bulb

at the stem base. This variety is grown for its stem, leaves and bulb. The licorice-flavored bulb is popular raw in salads, cooked in soups and stews or roasted like other root vegetables. Sweet, crunchy French hybrid **'Trieste'** does well in all kinds of weather. **'Solaris'** is a large, uniform selection, producing semi-flat bulbs that are vigorous and resistant to bolting. Large, bolt-resistant **'Zefa Fino'** is ready for harvest in 80 days. It bears flattish bulbs, green almost to the root. **'Orion'** is also ready in 80 days and has large, thick, rounded bulbs. It has a higher yield than open-pollinated varieties, a nice anise flavor and a crisp texture. **Var.** *dulce* (sweet fennel) bears green-brown seeds. **'Purpureum'** ('Atropurpureum'; bronze fennel) is similar in appearance to the species but has bronzy purple foliage. This cultivar is usually sold as an ornamental, but its parts are entirely edible.

Problems and Pests

Fennel rarely suffers from any problems.

Early Anglo Saxons believed fennel to be one of nine sacred herbs, capable of bestowing longevity, strength, courage and good eyesight.

Kale, Collards & Mustard Greens

Brassica

These leafy plants are some of the most decorative members of the Brassica family. This grouping is growing steadily in popularity, and for good reason. The nutrient content, flavor, texture and pure versatility are second to none. Mustards are most often eaten when quite young and lend a spicy flavor to stir-fries and salads. Collectively, this group is incredibly nutritious as well as delicious and is no longer used simply as a ho-hum garnish.

Young, purple mustard greens (above)

Starting

Sow seeds directly in the garden or set out transplants. These cool-season vegetables do well planted in fall in warmer areas; where winters are cool, plant in spring for an early-summer harvest. A light frost won't harm them and may even make them sweeter. Cover young plants if night-time temperatures are expected to drop to 15° F or lower. You may wish to make several successive plantings of mustard because the leaves have the best flavor when young and tender.

Growing

These plants grow best in **full sun** or **partial shade** in inland areas. The soil should be **fertile, moist** and **well drained**. Mustard in particular should not be allowed to dry out, or the leaves may become bitter.

'Tuscan' kale (above)

Green and purple kale ready for harvest (below)

Harvesting

Unlike their cousins broccoli and cauliflower, these plants do not form a head but instead send up a loose collection of large leaves. Start harvesting soon after planting by picking a few outer leaves from each plant.

Tips

These plants make a striking addition to beds and borders, where the foliage creates a good complement and backdrop for plants with brightly colored flowers. Full of vitamins A and C, the leaves make snappy additions to stir-fries and soups.

Recommended

B. oleracea **var.** *acephala* (collards; Scotch kale, curly-leaved kale) and *B. oleracea* **var.** *fimbriata* (Siberian

kale, Russian kale) are the kales and collards; however, the two common names are not used consistently.

Popular kale selections include the following. **'Blue Curled'** and **'Blue Ridge'** have good flavor and vigor. **'Improved Dwarf Siberian'** is ready in 50 days, maintaining its quality in the garden long after other selections have bolted. Disease-resistant **'Winter Red'** produces dark green, oak-shaped leaves with purple veins. The tender, sweet leaves are ready in 50 days, reaching 24–30 inches in height. A series of kales incredibly popular for their mild, crisp flavor, color variance, vigor and cold resistance includes **'Redbor,'** **'Winterbor'** and **'Ripbor.'** They're early, high-yielding heirloom selections. **'Red Russian'** is also an heirloom. It produces tender, sweet, green leaves with red spines. **'Curly Green'** is very curly,

Collards

green and great even when flowering. **'Tuscan'** ('Black Tuscany,' 'Lacinato,' 'Dinosaur', 'Nero di Toscano) is one of the tastiest and most ornamental forms. An heirloom, this cabbage cross bears long, strap-like, blistered, dark green to almost black leaves and is a true vegetable garden workhorse.

Popular collards include **'Top Bunch,'** a Georgia-type hybrid with large, slightly textured leaves, ready in 50 days. **'Flash'** is another early variety with smooth leaves. This selection is very slow to bolt and will continue to produce while the leaves are picked throughout the season. Bolt-resistant **'Hi-Crop'** has crinkled, blue-green, smooth leaves with a sweet flavor and is ready in 70 days. **'Blue Max'** is highly disease resistant and is ready in 70 days, while **'Champion'** is ready in 60 days, bearing rich green leaves in a compact form.

B. juncea **subsp.** *rugosa* (mustard) forms large clumps of ruffled, creased or wrinkled leaves in shades of green, blue-green, bronze or purple. **'Savanna'** produces large, thick, deep green leaves with a savory but mild flavor. **'Florida Broadleaf'** is an heirloom variety, producing

Robust, versatile kale shows up in many international dishes, such as the Irish side dish colcannon, a kale-potato combo, and Portuguese caldo verde soup, which mixes kale with spicy sausage, potatoes, broth and olive oil. Californians favor kale chips, which are lightly salted kale leaves tossed with olive oil and baked till crisp.

smooth leaves with white midribs. Ready in 45–50 days, this mustard has a sharp cabbage flavor when leaves are harvested young. **'Mizuna'** ('Japonica') is a Japanese mustard variety with finely cut, curled leaves with a pleasant, mild flavor. Ready in 65 days, this selection will continue to grow after being cut. **'Mibuna'** has lance-shaped leaves, mild flavor and is regarded as a cold-season vegetable. It is mature in 40 days, but the baby leaves can be harvested at 20 days. **'Red Giant'** produces brilliant maroon leaves with light green midribs. The leaves are spicy and flavorful and ready for harvest in 45 days. With a wasabi-like flavor, **'Spicy Green Mustard'** is an attention-getter with frilly leaves. Enjoy it in only 30 days.

Problems and Pests

Problems with cutworms, leaf miners, caterpillars, root maggots, cabbage white butterfly larvae, white rust, downy mildew and powdery mildew can occur.

Kale was the most widely consumed vegetable in Europe until the Middle Ages, when it was displaced by cabbage.

Kohlrabi

Brassica

The tender, swollen stem base of kohlrabi looks like something from outer space, making it very popular with children. The leaf base stretches as the bulb forms, and new leaves continue to sprout from the top of the rounded bulb. Adults and children enjoy this tasty turnip-like vegetable on salad and dinner plates.

Starting

Sow seed directly in the garden about 2 weeks after the last frost date. In areas with warm winters, sow again in fall. This plant matures quite quickly, so make several small sowings 1–2 weeks apart for a continuous supply of tender, young kohlrabi.

Growing

Kohlrabi grows best in **full sun**. The soil should be **fertile, moist** and **well drained**, though plants adapt to most moist soils. Encourage good growth by keeping soil moist, and harvest quickly once bulbs form.

Harvesting

Keep a close eye on your kohlrabi because bulbs become tough and woody quickly if left in the ground too long. Bulbs are well rounded and

Some people think kohlrabi is a magnet for insects that frequent other Brassicas, but a floating row cover atop your crop will reduce that threat.

2–4 inches in diameter when ready for harvesting. Pull up the entire plant and cut just below the bulb. Then cut leaves and stems off and compost or use to mulch the bed.

Tips

Low and bushy, with white or purple bulbs, kohlrabi makes an interesting edging plant for beds and borders and can be included in container gardens.

Recommended

B. oleracea subsp. *gongylodes* forms a low, bushy clump of blue-green foliage. As the plant matures, the stem just above ground level swells and becomes rounded. This is the edible part. '**Purple**' and '**White**' are common in seed catalogs and are the standard hybrids of the subspecies. They mature in 55 days, are very productive and are nutty in flavor without becoming woody.

More unique cultivars and hybrids are also available. **'Rapid Star'** bears rounded, pale green bulbs and is ready in 52 days. The **Vienna Series** includes **'White Vienna,'** which takes 56 days to produce light green to white bulbs with smooth skin and white flesh, and **'Purple Vienna,'** which is similar in every aspect but color. This series is known for its sweet flavor and tender texture, and the bulbs are ideal for freezing for later use. **'Granlibakken'** is an earlier variety, ready in 46 days. It bears light green, uniform, rounded bulbs with an extra-tender texture and super-sweet flavor. Early **'Korridor'** bears white bulbs with a rich flavor. Considered one of the best-tasting purple varieties, **'Kolibri'** is ready in 45 days.

Problems and Pests

Problems with cutworms, leaf miners, caterpillars, root maggots, cabbage white butterfly larvae, white rust, downy mildew and powdery mildew can occur.

The name comes from the German kohl *(cabbage) and* rabe *(turnip) because the plant is a cross between the two.*

Leeks

Allium

Leeks can rival most ornamental grasses for garden presence. The plants are strongly upright with stunning dark blue-green leaves that arch from the main stem. Planted in a small group, they are a welcome addition to any border.

Starting

Leeks can be sown directly in the garden. Because they take a long time to mature, however, you may want to start them indoors 8–10 weeks before planting outdoors. Once the stems reach the diameter of a pencil, transplant them to the garden, roughly 4–6 inches apart, in a trench 4 inches deep. To make transplanting easier, trim the roots by half; otherwise leave them intact.

To get off to a quicker start, purchase plants at a garden center or nursery. In areas with cool winters, set leeks out in spring; in warm winter regions, plant in fall.

Growing

Leeks grow best in **full sun**. The soil should be **fertile** and **well drained**, but plants adapt to most well-drained soils. Improve less-than-ideal soil by mixing in compost or adding a layer of compost mulch once you have

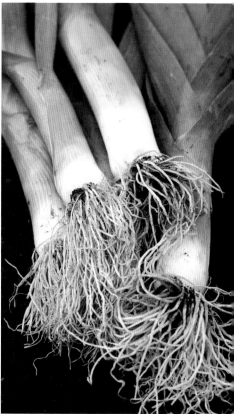

The leek is the national emblem of Wales, and Welsh people still wear one on their lapel on St. David's Day, March 1.

planted. Mounding mulch, soil or straw up around the base encourages white growth low on the plant.

Leeks favor cool, rainy regions but will adapt to other areas if given enough water.

Harvesting

Leeks can be harvested as soon as they mature, 4–7 months after planting, when stems are 1–2 inches in diameter. Dig them up gently with a garden fork. Harvest them as needed until the ground begins to freeze. In areas where winters are warm, simply leave them in the ground. These perennial plants will return year after year, and new seedlings grow in to replace fading plants.

Leeks keep for several weeks in the refrigerator if you cut the roots short and wrap the leeks in plastic. For longer storage, they can be frozen. Be sure to double bag so the onion-like flavor doesn't seep into any other food.

Tips

Leeks, with their bright blue-green leaves, are one of the most ornamental of all the onions. Plant them in groups in your beds and borders.

Recommended

A. ampeloprasum subsp. *porrum* is an upright perennial with blue-green leaves that cascade from the central stem. Globe-shaped clusters of flowers are borne atop a stem 36 inches tall the second year from planting. A wide array of hybrids and cultivars is available. '**Lancelot**' is ready in 90 days, producing bluish, erect foliage with bright white stalks that can reach up to 10 inches in height. This selection can be sown tightly together, without thinning, for a summer harvest of small, tender baby leeks. '**American Flag**' ('Broad London') is a mild leek, sweeter than onions. It grows to only 6 inches tall, matures firmly and is ready in 115 days. '**King Richard**' is an early variety, producing large leeks with white stems over 12 inches tall. '**Lincoln**' is a baby bunching variety, ready in 50 days, bearing tall, slender, tender scallion-like leeks. '**Bandit**' is winter-hardy, with dark blue-green, erect leaves ready in 120 days, with good uniformity, a thick shaft and a little bulbing at soil level. Dependable '**Electra**' has 7- to 8-inch shanks and is cold hardy. With large stalks 2 inches thick, '**Titan**' is ready to harvest in 110 days and has a mild flavor.

Problems and Pests

Problems with rot, mildew, smut, rust, leaf spot, onion flies and thrips can occur.

Leeks were once a popular cure for venomous bites, ulcers, nosebleeds, poor eyesight, drunkenness, toothaches, coughs, headaches and many other ills.

Lettuce & Mesclun

Letuca

With so many types of lettuce available, you never have to eat the same salad twice. Featuring undulating or rippled edges and variable leaf colors, lettuce is an ornamental treasure trove that deserves a spot in all types of gardens. The French term *mesclun* has come to mean a group of greens grown and harvested together. Many creative seed mixes are available. Whether the blend is spicy or mild, mesclun makes a welcome addition to salads and stir-fries while providing a good groundcover in the garden.

Starting

In areas where winters are cool, start lettuce and mesclun directly in the garden around the last frost date. Warm-winter regions enjoy two planting seasons—one in spring, the other in fall. Lettuce is sensitive to high temperatures and is often considered a cool-season crop. Planted in semi-shade, however, it is sometimes possible to get a summer crop of loose-leaf or mesclun.

When planting seeds of leaf lettuces and mesclun, make several smaller sowings 1–2 weeks apart for a continuous harvest. The seeds can be scattered across a prepared area and do not have to be planted in rows. Tuck mesclun under and around slower-growing vegetables like peppers and tomatoes. For head lettuces, which have a longer growing period, rows are preferable.

Growing

Lettuce and mesclun grow well in **full sun, light shade** or **partial shade** in a sheltered location. The soil should be **fertile, moist** and **well drained**. Add plenty of compost to improve the soil, and be sure to keep your lettuce moist.

Romaine lettuce (below)

Butterhead lettuce (above)

Lettuce is very prone to drying out in hot and windy situations, so it is best to plant it where it will get some protection. Plants under too much stress can quickly bolt and go to seed or simply wilt and die.

Harvesting

Head-forming lettuce can be harvested once the head is plump. If the weather turns very hot, you may wish to cut heads earlier because the leaves develop a bitter flavor once the plants go to flower.

Loose-leaf lettuce and mesclun can be harvested by pulling a few leaves off as needed or by cutting an entire plant 2–4 inches above ground level. Most leaf lettuces will continue to produce new leaves even if cut this way. Cut mesclun when it is about 4–5 inches tall; in 2 weeks, you'll have a new crop.

Tips

Lettuce and mesclun make interesting additions to container plantings, either alone or combined with other plants. In beds and borders, mesclun makes a decorative edging plant. All lettuces and mesclun are fairly low growing and should be planted near the front of a border so they will be easier to reach.

Recommended

L. sativa forms a clump of ruffle-edged leaves and comes in many forms.

Loose-leaf lettuce forms a loose rosette of leaves rather than a central head. A few of the many recommended loose-leaf varieties include the following. **'Grand Rapids'** is ready in 45 days, producing large, frilly, bright green leaves that are tender and sweet. This variety is vigorous and slower to bolt than its contemporaries. **'Prizehead'** produces loose, crumpled leaves

To add a twist to your purchased mesclun mixes, try adding a few herb seeds; cilantro, dill, parsley and basil are a few you may enjoy.

Loose-leaf lettuce (below)

edged with reddish brown in 45–55 days and has a buttery flavor. Slow-bolting **'Royal Oak'** has large, dark green leaves that are tender as baby leaves. **'Red Salad Bowl'** produces loose, deeply cut, deep burgundy leaves in a rosette form and is slow to bolt. The flavor is mild and non-bitter. One of the frilliest green oakleaf varieties, **'Tango'** looks outstanding in the salad bowl. Compact **'Dano,'** producer of the deepest oakleaf, is prized for its delicious

baby leaves. **'Simpson Elite'** is mature at 50 days but can be harvested at 30–45 days. It is incredibly vigorous, with a delicate flavor that rarely gets bitter. **'Mascara,'** a slow-to-bolt red oakleaf, tolerates heat and is gorgeous in the ornamental bed and on the plate.

Butterhead or Boston lettuce forms a loose head and has a very mild flavor. **'Butterhead'** and **'Dark Green Boston'** are reliable varieties. Slow-to-bolt **'Buttercrunch'** grows well year-round in many areas. Miniature **'Tom Thumb,'** about the size of a baseball, is ideal for containers. **'Bibb'** produces a loose head of buttery leaves with a distinctive flavor. This selection is early, maturing in 57 days. **'Esmeralda'** is considered a gourmet lettuce. It has a sweet flavor and succulent texture and is resistant to bolting and pests. Buy **'Drunken Woman Frizzy Headed'** lettuce for the name alone and also enjoy the 8-inch green plants with red edges.

Romaine or cos lettuce has a more upright habit, and the heads are fairly loose but cylindrical in shape. **'Baby Star'** is a mini romaine that is ready in 65–85 days, producing dark green, shiny leaves with a creamy white blanched heart. Ideal for home gardens, shapely, virus-resistant **'Parris Island'** grows to 11 inches tall. Dark green **'Valmaine'** produces heads 10 inches tall.

Crisphead or iceberg lettuce forms a very tight head of leaves and does well where temperatures are moderate but may be difficult in hot-summer areas. **'Early Great Lakes'** is ready in 65–85 days, depending on whether you harvest baby or mature leaves. **'Ithaca'** vigorously produces tightly wrapped, crisp heads.

Mesclun mixes often combine different lettuces, usually loose-leaf types, and are eaten while very young and tender. Mixes also include other species such as mustard, broccoli, radicchio, endive, arugula, chicory and spinach. Most seed catalogs offer a good selection of pre-mixed mesclun; you can also mix your own. The color and texture of the leaves are quite varied, making for a beautiful salad. **'Mild Mesclun'** has red and green leaf lettuces plus Asian greens; **'Misticanza'** includes 14 Italian lettuces.

Problems and Pests

Problems with root rot, leaf spot, flea beetle and mosaic virus can occur.

Okra

Abelmoschus

Native to Asia, okra is a heavy producer often fried or used in soups and stews. Grown in summer, okra sports beautiful flowers similar to those of its cousin, hibiscus.

Starting

Okra germinates quickly in warm soil. Soak seeds overnight before planting to improve germination. In warmer areas, direct sow in spring. Otherwise, start them in peat pots 6–8 weeks before you plan to move them to the garden. Wait until after the last frost date and the soil has warmed before moving them outside.

Growing

Okra grows best in **full sun** in a sheltered location. The soil should be **fertile, moist** and **well drained**. Okra likes hot growing conditions, so plant it in the hottest part of your garden, and use plenty of mulch to conserve water. Stake the 4- to 5-foot-tall plants.

The red stems and upright form are quite stunning mixed in with ornamental plants (below).

'Cajun Delight' (above)

Harvesting

This plant can be spiny, so it is best to wear gloves when harvesting. Pick fruit when it is still immature, about 3–4 inches long, usually 1–2 weeks after the flower drops and the pod sets. Okra grows fast; pick pods every 2–3 days, and keep the pods picked, or the plant will stop bearing.

Tips

Okra makes an attractive addition to container plantings. Extend your growing season by bringing the entire container indoors when cool weather or frost is expected.

Recommended

A. esculentus is a bushy, upright plant with sometimes spiny foliage and brown- or purple-spotted, yellow, hibiscus-like flowers. Flowers are borne at the base of each leaf. Plants mature about 50 days after transplant. **'Cajun Delight'** and **'Dwarf Green'** are two of the more common varieties available. **'Red Burgundy,'** a 2010 All-America Selections winner, is ready in 85 days, bearing deep red stems, branches and leaf mid-ribs. The fruits grow 6–8 inches long when mature, resulting in tender pods that turn a deep green when cooked. **'Clemson Spineless,'** also an All-America Selections winner, is ready in 56 days, producing tender, rich green pods 6 inches long. The pods are pointed and slightly grooved. Heirloom **'Alabama Red'** produces fat, red pods. **'Blondy'** is mature at 48 days in an open-pollinated form. It grows

into a compact, 36-inch-tall plant, bearing heaps of pods.

Problems and Pests

Occasional problems with slugs, spider mites, whiteflies, cabbage white butterfly larvae, fungal leaf spot or powdery mildew can occur.

Okra is a love-it or hate-it type of vegetable. It has a slimy texture when cooked, and a flavor described as "a mix between green beans and oysters." Fans love it battered and fried.

Onions

Allium

One of the oldest cultivated plants, onions have been grown for 5000 years—so long that we have forgotten their origin. We do know that ancient Greeks, Romans and Egyptians all grew and ate onions in great abundance. Californians find them well worth growing as well. Try them in your garden. Many of the more interesting and flavorful varieties aren't available in the supermarket.

Starting

Start from seed indoors 6–8 weeks before planting outdoors; they can also be sown directly in the garden once the last frost date has passed. When sowing onion seed, place 2–3 seeds per inch in rows ½ inch deep. Thin seedlings when they reach 2 inches tall, leaving a seedling every 1–2 inches. The onions you pulled can be used as green onions, or scallions.

For a faster start, plant onion sets—small bulbs less than 1 inch wide.

Bunching onions are usually started from seed sown directly in the garden. They are quick to mature, so make several smaller sowings 2–3 weeks apart from spring to midsummer for a regular supply.

Onions make interesting additions to container plantings, particularly those close to the house so you can conveniently pick a few while cooking.

Growing

Onions need **full sun**. The soil should be **fertile, moist** and **well drained**. Onions use plenty of water but will rot in very wet soil. They are poor at competing with other plants, so keep them well weeded. A good layer of mulch will conserve moisture and keep the weeds down. Be sure to water during periods of extended drought.

Harvesting

All onions can be harvested and used as needed throughout the season. For green onions, pull up those that need thinning. Pinch back the tops if you want the bulbs to mature or the plant to continue to produce leaves.

Bulb onions grown for storage are ready for harvest when the leaves begin to yellow and flop and the shoulders of the bulbs are just visible above the soil line. Pull and dry them for a few days before storing them in a dry, cold, frost-free spot.

Onions are perennials and can be left in the ground over winter, though the flavor can become quite strong the second year. They will flower the second summer.

Tips

Onions have fascinating cylindrical leaves that add an interesting vertical accent to the garden. Include them in beds and borders, but if you want big bulbs, don't crowd them with other plants. If you want small bulbs, pack them in.

Egyptians regarded the onion as a symbol of eternity, and buried them with their pharaohs.

'Evergreen' (below)

Recommended

A. cepa (bulb onion) forms a clump of cylindrical foliage and develops a large, round or flattened bulb. Bulb formation is day-length dependent. The Vegetable Research and Information Center at the University of California at Davis recommends that those who live north of Bakersfield plant early types in November through January for spring and summer harvest, and late types from January

through March for summer and fall harvest. If you garden south of Bakersfield, plant early varieties in October and harvest in June. Late varieties are not recommended in the south. Long-day (late) cultivars include heirloom **'Southport White Globe,'** a versatile, cold-tolerant onion that thrives in all areas; **'Stockton,'** a reliable grower popular in the Sacramento area that is available in red, white and yellow; and **'Ailsa Craig,'** a huge, yellow, sweet Spanish type that garnishes many sandwiches. Short-day (early) recommendations include slow-bolting **'California Early Red,'** great for salads and cooking; **'Granex,'** a semi-flat, sweet hybrid that can reach 5 inches in diameter; and **'Grano,'** a medium,

red or white onion with superior versatility.

A. fistulosum (bunching onion, green onion, scallion) is a perennial that forms a clump of foliage. The plant quickly begins to divide and multiply from the base. Plants may develop small bulbs or no bulbs at all. Once established, these plants will provide you with onions all spring and summer. **'Evergreen'** is ready in 60–75 days. This selection was bred for its crisp, deep green, rich, mild-tasting foliage. For something a little different, **'Salad Apache'** is a deep purple variety bearing deep purple-red–skinned ends in 80 days. The flavor is mild, and the texture is crisp. The purple outer skin blends with shades of silver when peeled, adding contrast and a little color to your cooking. This is a great bunching onion to grow in containers. **'Red Baron'** is a later bunching onion, ready in 105–115 days. It produces high yields of intense red and green roots and thrives in high-density plantings.

A. oschaninii and *A. ascalonicum* are the two species of perennials known as shallots. *A. oschaninii* is considered to be the "true" shallot species that comes from Central to Southwest Asia. *A. ascalonicum* is more of an Indian species, equally as common and delicious. Like garlic, shallots are formed in offsets, or clusters, making up a head of multiple cloves. The skin color ranges from golden brown to rosy red to gray, and the white flesh can be tinged with green or pink. Shallots are firm and sweeter than other onions, yet pungent. They are also smaller—much smaller than a bulb onion but larger than the root end of a scallion. **'Banana'** is an unusual, long shallot with shiny, copper-brown skin, crisp, white flesh and a very distinctive flavor, ready in 85 days. **'Picador'** is a rounded shallot with brownish pink skin, white flesh tinged with pink and a unique, mild flavor, ready in 88 days. This selection is considered to be a French shallot.

Problems and Pests

Problems with smut, onion maggots and rot can occur.

"Knowing your onions" is an old phrase referring to the more than 400 Allium species, including leeks, chives, garlic, shallots and many forms of onion.

Parsnips

Pastinaca

A root vegetable related to the carrot, parsnip imparts
a smooth, sweet earthy flavor to soups and stews.
Rich in potassium, it is also delicious peeled and
roasted with a sprinkle of olive oil and salt.
Parsnip has not reached its full potential
in the states, though Europeans
have enjoyed this vegetable since
the days of the Roman Empire.

Starting

Where winters are cold, sow seeds in spring. In warm winter regions, plant in fall. Cold makes parsnips sweeter. Roots may grow as deep as 15 inches, so make sure your soil is well cultivated. Soak seeds for 24 hours before planting to improve germination.

Growing

Parsnips grow best in **full sun** but tolerate some light shade. The soil should be of **average fertility, moist** and **well drained**. Be sure to work the soil well and mix in compost to improve the texture. Roots develop poorly in heavy soil. Mulch to suppress weed growth and to conserve moisture. Big, spreading parsnip tops take up a lot of room, so plan accordingly.

To avoid "hairy roots," do not use manure as a fertilizer. A bed that contains manure from the previous year, however, should be fine.

Harvesting

Pull roots in fall or spring, depending on planting time. Frost improves flavor because some of the root starches are converted to sugar in freezing weather, resulting in a sweeter vegetable.

Roasting the roots brings out their sweetness. Combine parsnips with potatoes, carrots and other root vegetables, then drizzle with oil and sprinkle with herbs before roasting for an hour, or until the vegetables are tender.

Parsnips can be pulled from the garden all winter in areas where the ground does not freeze solid.

Tips

Not the most ornamental of vegetables, parsnips provide a dark, leafy background to low-growing plants and produce plenty of vegetables for very little effort.

Recommended

P. sativa is an upright plant with dark green, divided leaves. It develops a long, pale creamy yellow root that looks like a carrot. Heirloom **'All-American'** is ready to harvest in 95–105 days, earlier than other varieties. **'Harris Model'** yields 15-inch-long parsnips with a sweet,

nut-like flavor and is ready in 130 days. Mild, white-fleshed **'Hollow Crown'** produces 12-inch-long results in 105 days. **'Javelin'** is a smooth-skinned parsnip that is resistant to canker. The uniform roots have great flavor, and the roots keep well in the soil for fall and winter harvest. **'Excalibur'** is a later variety, ready in 180 days. It produces smooth, almost bleached white roots with creamy flesh and sweet flavor. The roots have shallow crowns, which is great for later crops. **'Gladiator'** is considered to be the best hybrid parsnip for its consistently high quality, silky smooth skin and true parsnip flavor. **'Arrow'** is an earlier variety producing large, uniform roots in great abundance with a sweet, delicate flavor and tender texture. **'Tender & True'** is an heirloom variety ready in 105 days. It is an open-pollinated parsnip, bearing long, canker-resistant roots.

Problems and Pests

Canker, carrot rust flies and onion maggots can affect parsnips.

This cousin of the carrot was once prescribed as a treatment for ulcers, colic, pain, consumption, snakebites and psychological ills.

Peas

Pisum

It's easy to love peas. They are simple to grow (as long as the weather is cool), versatile, tasty and easy to store. Whether you long for the fresh flavor of shelling peas or the satisfying crunch of snap peas, they will grow well in California provided you plant to take advantage of cool temperatures. In some areas, you may get two crops.

Starting

Peas show an admirable appreciation for cool weather. Where winters are cold, you may get two crops by planting in early spring and again in fall about 12 weeks before the first frost. In regions with warm winters, plant in fall. Peas mature in 60–70 days; count backward to make sure they don't ripen in the heat of summer.

Peas, like beans, can be treated with bacterial inoculant before planting to ensure a good supply of nitrogen-fixing bacteria on the roots.

Growing

Peas grow well in **full sun**. The soil should be **average to fertile, humus rich, moist** and **well drained**.

Both bush and vining peas are available. Bush types do not need support. For vining peas, provide support such as twiggy branches, nets or chain link fences for their small, twining tendrils. Base your support height on the expected height of the plants, and make sure it is in place before your seeds sprout because the roots are quite shallow and can be damaged easily. Bush types do well in most areas of the state; vining types are particularly successful along the coast due to cooler temperatures.

Harvesting

Harvest peas when they are still young and tender. They can be pulled from the vine by hand, but use both hands—one to hold the plant and one to pull the pea pod—to avoid damaging the plant. The more

Snap peas

you pick, the more peas the plants will produce.

Tips

Peas make excellent privacy plants. They will grow easily up a low chain-link fence, and the taller varieties create a privacy screen quite quickly. The shorter and medium-height peas make interesting additions to hanging baskets and container plantings. They grow up hangers or supports and can also spill over edges and trail down.

Peas have been cultivated for so many generations that their birthplace is unknown. There is, however, a legend that states that peas came from Thor, the Norse god of thunder. It was said that Thor sent peas crashing to the earth to plug up humans' wells, but a few missed the mark and rooted instead.

Recommended

P. sativum var. sativum is a climbing plant with bright green, waxy stems and leaves and white flowers. The resulting pods are grouped into three categories: shelling (English, garden) peas, snow (sugar) peas and snap (sugar snap) peas. The seeds are removed from the pods of shelling peas and are the only part eaten. Snow peas are eaten as flat, almost seedless pods, often including the edible vine tips and newest leaves. Snap peas develop fat seeds, and the pod and seeds are eaten together. There is a wide array of varieties to choose from, but here are a few from each category.

Shelling pea varieties include small bush types such as **'Alaska,'** one of the oldest peas available. It is a heavy producer, bearing 2- to 3-inch-long pods in 50–55 days, and is resistant to cold, pests and wilt. **'Early Freezer'** is ready in 58 days,

bearing double-podded peas, ranging from 7 to 8 peas in each 3-inch-long pod. **'Green Arrow'** is an heirloom shelling pea, boasting high yields, 4-inch-long pods and an average of 9–11 peas per pod. This tender pea requires no support, is ready in 58–63 days and is highly disease tolerant. **'Paladio'** produces big, easy-to-open pods. This variety is often borne in doubles, making for easy picking and shelling.

Vining selections include **'Laxton's Progress,'** a vigorous dwarf vine with 4- to 5-inch-long pods, and **'Little Marvel,'** with peas that hold well on the vine. Larger vining types include vigorous, sweet **'Freezonian,'** with 30-inch-tall vines and 3½-inch-long pods with 7–8 peas each; **'Green Marvel,'** a disease-resistant variety with double pods and 24-inch-tall vines; and productive, disease-resistant **'Maestro,'** also with 24-inch-tall vines.

Snow peas are equally as varied. **'Snow Green'** has dark green,

3-inch-long pods that are borne in multiples. The plants do not need support and are resistant to disease. **'Mammoth Melting'** is an heirloom variety that produces huge, long, edible pods with a sweet, mild flavor. **'Oregon Sugar Pod II'** is a heavy yielder, producing tender, flat, 10-inch-long pods. This dwarf plant produces peas ready for harvest in 60 days. **'Oregon Giant'** is very similar but more uniform with larger pods, and takes a little longer to mature.

For snap, or sugar snap, **'Sugar Ann'** is an All-America Selections winner and is ready for harvest in 75 days. It bears rounded, fleshy pods on vines that can reach up to 36 inches tall. Sweet, stringless **'Sugar Lace'** is self-supporting, only

15½ inches tall with 3-inch-long pods. **'Sugar Snap Cascadia'** is a dwarf variety ready for harvest in 70 days, bearing fleshy, crisp, sweet, rounded pods that remain tender and sweet for a long period, particularly compared to other varieties. It is also resistant to pea wilt. **'Sugar Daddy'** is a cross between a shelling pea and a snow pea that results in a sugarless snap pea. Bearing nearly twice as much as other varieties, disease-resistant **'Super Sugar Snap'** has plump pods and great flavor.

Problems and Pests

Peas are prone to powdery mildew, so choose mildew-resistant varieties, plant in full sun, and avoid touching the plants when they are wet to prevent the spread of disease. Aphids and whiteflies can also cause problems.

Smooth-seeded varieties are starchier and best used for soups, while wrinkled varieties are sweeter and generally eaten fresh.

Peppers

Capsicum

The variety of sweet and chili peppers is nothing short of remarkable. Among the many different shapes, colors and flavors of peppers, there is sure to be one or two that appeal to you. The high cost of bell peppers at the market encourages many California gardeners to grow their own, and nothing beats a home-grown chili or Italian roasting pepper in the many ethnic dishes we deliver direct from our kitchens.

'Habanero' (above)

Starting

Peppers need warmth to germinate
and grow. Start seeds indoors
6–10 weeks before the last frost date.
Plant seedlings or purchased container plants outside in a warm,
sunny location when temperatures
remain above 50° F.

Growing

Peppers grow best in **full sun** in
a warm location. The soil should be
average to fertile, moist and **well
drained**. Mulch to keep them moist.
Peppers need heat to thrive and can
dry out quickly, yet if they get too
much heat, they may stop growing
until the temperature drops. It's an
adventure!

*Pepper heat is rated on scale of 1–10
or by Scoville units. Sweet peppers
have about 100 Scoville units, while
habaneros can have up to 350,000.*

Harvesting

For the fullest flavor, pick peppers when ripe. If you need to pick them early, they will continue ripening after they've been picked. Chili peppers can also be dried.

Tips

Pepper plants are neat and bushy. Once the peppers set and begin to ripen, the plants can be very color-ful as the bright red, orange and yellow fruits contrast beautifully with the dark green foliage. They are a worthwhile addition to a hot, sunny border, even if you don't care to eat peppers.

All peppers are good additions to container plantings. Chili peppers in particular are useful in containers because they usually have the most

interesting fruit shapes. Some of the smaller chili peppers also make interesting houseplants for warm, sunny windows.

Recommended

C. annuum is the most common species of sweet and chili peppers. Plants are bushy with dark green foliage. Flowers are white, and peppers can be shades of green, red, orange, yellow, purple or brown.

Cultivars of sweet peppers include crisp, thick-fleshed **'California Wonder,'** with a mild, pleasant flavor. If you have a short growing season, try early **'King of the North'** for big 4- to 6-inch, red peppers in 68 days. One of the finest purple varieties, **'Purple Beauty'** is only 17 inches tall yet produces abundant 3-inch fruit. Highly disease resistant, pretty **'Blushing Beauty'** goes from ivory to blush to red and can be harvested

'Scotch Bonnet' (above)

Capsaicin is the chemical that gives peppers their heat. It is also the chemical used in pepper spray.

at any stage. Bull's horn variety **'Carmen,'** a 2006 All-American Selections winner, ripens in 75 days and has thick walls. Lovely **'Orange Sun'** matures in 80 days with 4- to 5-inch fruit.

Some of the most tasty and beautiful sweet peppers are found in seed catalogs. **'Mini Belle'** mix is ready in 90 days on dwarf, compact plants that produce large yields of small, blocky, sweet bell peppers in red, orange, purple or brown. This mix is ideal for containers. **'Big Bertha'** is a sweet bell pepper that produces jumbo fruits that change from green to red with maturity. Popular hybrid **'Jingle Bell'** features tiny 1½-inch, sweet peppers that change from green to red. They're great for appetizers and stir-fries.

Cultivars of chili peppers include **'Anaheim,' 'Cayenne,' 'Jalapeno,'**

'**Scotch Bonnet**' and '**Thai,**' just to name a few.

Serrano-type '**Huasteco**' is longer and thicker than others of this variety and has good disease resistance.

Sweet banana peppers, or Hungarian wax peppers, are another group, more sweet than hot. They are elongated, often in bright shades of yellow and orange. '**Banana**' is an All-America Selections winner ready in 70 days and is sweet, with no trace of heat. It can be harvested at any size but is best at 5–6 inches long. The fruits are pale yellow when ripe and are vigorously produced. Heirloom '**Balloon**' features small, unusual bell-shaped fruit that is both sweet (flesh) and hot (seeds).

C. chinense '**Habanero**' is one of the hottest chili peppers. It is native to the Caribbean. '**Naga Jolokia**' ('Bhut Jolokia') is believed to be the world's hottest pepper. It is ready for harvest in 150 days, has Indian origins and is best sown indoors 8–10 weeks before the last frost to ensure fruit. '**Naga Jolokia Chocolate**' is similar but is dark reddish brown with a slightly mottled or rough-textured skin.

Problems and Pests

Rare problems with aphids and whiteflies can occur.

Pepper breeding is an incredibly competitive industry. Breeders from all over the world continue to try to produce the hottest pepper ever, even beyond what is currently the hottest, the 'Naga Jolokia.'

Potatoes

Solanum

Potatoes were cultivated in South America for centuries before the Spanish brought them to Europe. In turn, Europeans helped North America jump on the spud wagon. Today, heirloom varieties are in fashion, mixing it up with newer cultivars fancy and plain, small and large; no matter what new varieties come out, the heirloom potatoes are often the best and have stood the test of time.

Hill up the soil at the base of the plants as the potatoes mature to block out any light.

Starting

Start your potato crop by purchasing sets of seed potatoes (small tubers). Plant in spring a few weeks before the last frost date, as long as the soil isn't too cold and wet. Young plants can tolerate a light frost, but not a hard freeze. Seed potatoes can be cut into smaller pieces, as long as each one has an "eye," the dimpled spot from which the plant and roots grow. Each piece needs 12–18 inches of growing space.

Potatoes are a cool-season crop. When you plant depends on your geographic region. The University of California Vegetable Research and Information Center offers this guide for planting: Monterey County and north, March through June; San Luis Obispo County and south, March through May, July through August; Interior valleys, December through March, July through August;

All parts of the potato plant are **poisonous** *except the tubers, and they can become poisonous if exposed to light. Green flesh is a good indication that this has occurred. To protect them, mound soil around plants, an inch or so per week, from midsummer to fall. Straw mulch also effectively shades developing tubers.*

and Imperial and Coachella valleys, November through January.

Growing

Potatoes prefer **full sun** but tolerate some shade. The soil should be **fertile, humus rich, acidic, moist** and **well drained**, though potatoes adapt to most growing conditions and tolerate both hot and cold weather. Mound soil up around the plants to keep the tubers out of the light as they develop. Potatoes have shallow root systems and should be kept moist.

Harvesting

Harvest potatoes 2–4 months after planting. Tubers begin to form around the same time the plants

begin to flower. Dig up a few tubers at a time as you need them.

For long-term storage, dig them up and let them dry for a few hours on the soil, and then brush the dirt off and store the tubers in a cold, dark place. You can save a few of the smaller ones for planting the following spring. If you live in a no-frost area, you can leave potatoes in the ground until you need them.

Tips

These large, bushy plants with white, pink or light purple flowers are good fillers for an immature border and are excellent at breaking up soil in newer gardens.

Recommended

S. tuberosum is a bushy, mound-forming plant. It bears tiny, exotic-looking, white, pink or light purple flowers

Is your potato high or low in starch? To find out, cut one in half, rub the cut surfaces together and stick them together as if you were reassembling the potato. If they stick, the starch content is high. High-starch varieties are better for baking and mashing. Low-starch spuds are better for boiling and potato salad.

in late summer. There are many varieties of potatoes available. They can have rough or smooth, white, yellow, brown, red or blue skin and white, yellow, purple or blue flesh. A few popular varieties include **'All-Blue,'** with smooth, blue skin and light purple-blue flesh; **'Nooksack,'** a good performer in wet areas; **'Norgold Russet,'** a fine baking potato; **'Norland,'** with smooth, red skin and white flesh; **'White Superior,'** an early white variety; and **'Yukon Gold,'** with smooth, light beige skin and yellow flesh.

Beyond the more traditional, well-known varieties are some of the more unusual and fun ones. **'Kennebec'** is slowly on its way to becoming a commonly known spud because of its high yield potential of oblong tubers and its disease and drought tolerance. **'Burbank Russet'** is a large, flat, white-fleshed variety with shallow eyes. This potato has a great

'Kennebec' (above)

shelf life and is best grown in light, sandy soil. **'Banana'** is a fingerling type with yellow skin and flesh. Its vigorous growth results in heavy yields. **'Austrian Crescent'** is another fingerling variety, with tan skin and yellow flesh. **'Purple Peruvian'** is also a fingerling, but it is purple inside and out. **'Caribe'** produces a purple skin with pure white flesh in mid-season.

Problems and Pests

Potatoes are susceptible to a variety of diseases, including scab. Avoid planting them in the same spot 2 years in a row. Potato beetle is the most troublesome insect pest.

Purchase seed sets rather than trying to grow potatoes from the grocery store. Market potatoes may have been treated to prevent sprouting, or may be poorly suited to growth in your area.

Radishes

Raphanus

Radishes are grouped into two categories. Spring radishes, which include the familiar round, red and icicle types, are used in salads. Winter radishes, which include Oriental or daikon radishes and Spanish types, are eaten raw, cooked or pickled. The pods of some Oriental radishes are also popular in salads. Radishes are a great spicy addition to a variety of recipes far beyond the standard salad, so expand your vegetable garden and culinary horizons and give them a try.

Starting

In cool winter areas, start seeds in spring, as soon as the soil warms up a bit and can be worked. Warmer areas may get two crops—one planted in spring, the other in fall. Plants tolerate light frost. Successive, smaller plantings can be made every 2 weeks to ensure a steady supply. Mix fast-growing radishes with slower-growing vegetables such as carrots and get twice the yield from your garden.

Growing

Radishes grow well in **full sun** or **light shade**. The soil should be of **average fertility, loose, humus rich, moist** and **well drained**. Heavy or rocky soils cause rough, woody and unpleasant-tasting roots. Radishes sprout and mature quickly; some varieties are ready to harvest within 1 month.

Harvesting

Harvest spring radishes 3 weeks to 2 months after planting, as soon as the roots develop. Flavor and texture deteriorate quickly if they are left in the ground or stored for too long.

Daikon and Spanish radishes can be stored like carrots, in moist sand in a cool, dry location. They can also be pickled.

Tips

Easy to grow and a great addition to salads, radishes are also effective nurse plants. If planted with mature plants or those that are slow to germinate, such as parsnips and carrots,

Radishes tend to bolt in hot weather, causing the roots to develop an unpleasantly hot flavor.

Radishes are related to cabbage, broccoli and mustard.

radishes will shade out weeds and reduce evaporation.

Because of their leafy, low-growing habit, these plants make interesting edging plants for borders and are unique additions to container plantings. Use radishes for a quick-growing spring display that will eventually be replaced by other plants.

Recommended

R. sativus forms a low clump of leaves. The edible roots can be long and slender or short and round; the skin can be rosy red, purple, green, white or black. The following are some of the more standard selections. **'Cherry Belle'** is an extra-early variety with exceptionally short tops and bright red skin. **'China Rose'** and **'China White'** ('China Celestial') are from a series that dates back to the 18th century and were grown by

Thomas Jefferson at Monticello. This series produces roots 6–8 inches long, 2 inches in diameter, with smooth skin and crisp white flesh. **'French Breakfast'** is a large, scarlet radish, oblong in shape with white tips. The flesh is crisp, juicy, mild and sweet. It is ready in 20 days. **'Sparkler'** is ready in 25 days, bearing white roots that change to pink closer to the leafy stems.

Novelty radishes, including the following, are becoming more popular. **'Black Spanish Round'** produces round roots, 3–4 inches or larger,

The greens, or tops, of most radish selections can be eaten just like beet tops or turnip tops. They're tasty fresh or steamed and are full of nutrients.

Young daikon radishes (below)

with crisp, white, spicy flesh and black skin. This hardy cultivar is an excellent keeper. It is ready for harvest in 53 days. Heirloom **'Long Black Spanish'** is rarer than the rounded type but is highly sought after for its great flavor. It bears a root 9 inches long with blackish gray skin and pure white flesh that is pungent, spicy hot and crisp. A rare Chinese variety, **'Green Luobo'** is a green radish inside and out. It is an elongated type that is vigorous and quite large, with tender, moderately hot flesh. **'Mantanghong'** ('Beauty Heart') produces white-skinned, round radishes with bright purple flesh. The flesh is crisp, sweet and slightly nutty, and only slightly hot. This Chinese variety is often used as a garnish, carved into flower shapes. **'Red Meat'** ('Watermelon') is another Chinese radish, with white and green skin and dark pinkish red flesh. Sweet with a touch of heat, this 4-inch round radish resembles

the interior of a watermelon when sliced. For easy mixed color, try red, white and purple **'Easter Egg II,'** and mild, white-fleshed **'Purple Plum.'**

R. sativus var. *longipinnatus* (daikon radish) varieties are as delicious and interesting as the more standard radish selections. They are milder in flavor than black types, and larger than red and white types. Japanese **'New Crown'** is considered to be a deluxe variety of daikon. It grows 12–14 inches long and 2 inches wide, with snow white skin and pale green tops. **'White Icicle'** is an early daikon radish, ready in 20–30 days, bearing long, slender, white roots from tip to stem. **'Minowase Japanese'** ('Minowase Summer Cross') is ready in 50 days, producing white, tapered roots 8–10 inches long with a medium to hot flavor. **'Omny'** is ready in 60 days and grows 10–16 inches long. This selection is very slow to bolt and likes cool temperatures.

Problems and Pests

Flea beetles and cabbage maggots are common problems for radishes.

The Greeks held radishes in such high regard that they made gold replicas of them.

Rhubarb

Rheum

Like tomatoes, pumpkin and peppers, rhubarb treads the fine line between fruit and vegetable. We usually eat it in fruit dishes, but rhubarb is actually a vegetable. Because it benefits from winter chill, rhubarb can be challenging to grow in southern coastal areas. The leaves are poisonous.

Starting

Start plants in winter or early spring; warm-area gardeners should plant in fall. Rhubarb can be started from seed sown directly in the garden, but it will take a long time for the plant to be useable. Instead, look for crowns at the nursery or ask friends for a division.

Growing

Rhubarb grows best in **full sun** or **partial shade** in warmer areas. The soil should be **fertile, humus rich, moist** and **well drained**, but this plant adapts to most conditions. Gently work some compost into the soil around the rhubarb each year, and add a layer of compost mulch. Fertile soil encourages more and bigger stems. Remove flowers quickly; plants that flower produce fewer plants the following year.

Rhubarb can stay in one spot for many years but will remain more vigorous and productive if divided every 8 years. To rejuvenate the plant, dig it up in early spring while it is still dormant. Don't worry about severing large roots when removing the rootball from the ground. Using a knife or spade, divide the crown, or the top of the rootball, into several sections, such as into fourths or even smaller, making sure that each section contains at least one bud or "eye." Replant the sections into different locations. If you can't replant the sections immediately, store them in the refrigerator and rehydrate them by soaking them in a bucket of water for at least 6 hours before planting.

Although the flowers are quite interesting and attractive, you can remove them to prolong the stem harvest.

'Victoria' (above)

Only the stems of rhubarb are edible.
The leaves contain oxalic acid in toxic
quantities.

Harvesting

Begin picking rhubarb once stalks
are large enough to use and roughly
the width of your finger. Harvest
stems by pulling firmly and cleanly
from the base of the plant.

Do not harvest the stalks in the first
year. Let the plant develop an established root system first. Harvest
sparingly the second year—not more
than half of the stalks. In the third
and subsequent years, harvest freely.

Tips

Sadly, this stunning plant is often
relegated to back corners and waste
areas in the garden. With its dramatic
leaves, bright red stems and intriguing flowers, rhubarb deserves a far
more central location in a permanent
planting bed.

Recommended

R. rhabarbarum and **R. × hybridum**
form large clumps of glossy, deeply
veined, green, bronzy or reddish
leaves. The edible stems can be green,
red or a bit of both. Spikes of densely
clustered, red, yellow or green flowers
are produced in midsummer. A few

of the more popular varieties include **'Crimson Cherry,'** a vigorous type with bright red stalks on a plant 24–36 inches tall. Topping out at 36 inches, **'Victoria'** is an intensely colored variety that bears greenish leaf stalks that mature to a combination of red and green. It can be pulled after one year. **'Valentine'** is excellent for home gardeners, and its thick red stalks retain their color when cooked.

There is a wide variety of hybrids and cultivars to choose from, but here are a few that are known for unique characteristics. **'German Wine'** bears green petioles, similar to 'Victoria,' but 'German Wine' is more vigorous and intense in color, usually resulting in green stalks with dark pink speckling. **'Mammoth Red'** ('The Giant,' 'Stott's Mammoth,' 'Mammoth') is a vigorous producer, resulting in plants 4–5 feet tall, deep red stalks and large, green leaves. **'Sunrise'** is a pink variety with thick stalks, ideal for forcing.

Problems and Pests

Rhubarb rarely suffers from any problems.

Rutabagas & Turnips

Brassica

Among the tastiest of root vegetables, rutabagas and turnips are not as popular as they deserve to be. Try them in soups and stews and enjoy their warm, buttery flavor. They are also delicious roasted with other root vegetables, drizzled with a bit of olive oil.

Starting

Sow seeds directly in the garden in spring. In warm areas, plant in fall for winter harvest. Keep the seedbed moist until the plants germinate. Young plants can also be purchased at your local garden center and planted after last frost.

Plant turnips 6–8 inches apart, but give rutabagas more space because they're in the garden longer and may need a little more room to grow.

Growing

Rutabagas and turnips prefer to grow in **full sun**. The soil should be **fertile, moist** and **well drained**. Roots can develop discolored centers in boron-deficient soil. Work agricultural boron into the soil if needed. These plants require consistent moisture during the growing season to produce high-quality vegetables.

Harvesting

The leaves can be harvested a few at a time from each plant as needed and steamed or added to stir-fries, or eaten fresh when young and tender. At whatever stage they're harvested, they are best cooked. Try them with mustard or Swiss chard leaves.

The roots can be used as soon as they are plump and round, or leave them in the ground to sweeten during cooler weather. Dig them up, cut off the greens and let them dry just enough so the dirt can be brushed off. Store them in moist sand in a cold, frost-free location for winter. Turnips do not store as well or as long as rutabagas.

Turnips are strong, resilient plants, but don't let them dry out for long periods, as this will adversely affect the quality of the roots and the leaves.

Tips

Both rutabagas and turnips produce large, bushy clumps of blue-green foliage and can be included in the middle of a border. Though not particularly showy, they provide an attractive, contrasting background for other plants.

Recommended

B. napus (rutabaga, swede, winter turnip, yellow turnip) forms a large clump of smooth, waxy, blue-green leaves. The roots are most often white with purple tops, and most have yellow flesh, but white-fleshed varieties are available. Rutabagas are generally larger than turnips and take longer to mature. Choose a variety that is clubroot resistant, if this disease is common in your region. '**Laurentian**' and its many variations produce 6-inch roots.

They are commonly available and are popular because they store well. **'Laurentian Golden'** has smooth skin and light yellow flesh and is a good keeper. **'Joan'** has a fine texture, sweet flavor and resistance to clubroot. **'Marian'** is a vigorous grower with short, wide leaves for closer spacing. **'Magres'** is known for its delicious, rich flavor, and **'Virtue'** has red skin and sweet, yellow flesh. Nearly round, **'American Purple Top'** is a common variety with sweet, fine-grained, yellow flesh and will grow to 5 inches but is even tastier when harvested at 2–3 inches. The flesh turns bright orange when cooked. **'Helenor'** is a strong producer with golden flesh and red-skinned shoulders. **'Wilhelmsburger'** ('German Green Top') is a vigorous, disease-resistant heirloom variety with golden flesh and green shoulders. **'York'** is good for storing and is clubroot resistant.

There are turnip varieties grown for nothing but their edible greens.

B. rapa (turnip, summer turnip) isa biennial, very close to rutabaga in appearance. It often produces a large, rounded root but is also available in smaller varieties. The root, or swelling, grows at the surface of the soil with the top third exposed above ground level.

This top is often purple-skinned, while the bottom two-thirds is white. The flesh is often white or yellowish white. The leaves are rougher and hairier than rutabaga leaves. **'Early Purple Top White Globe'** and **'White Lady'** are popular cultivars. **'Just Right'** is ready in 70 days, producing white roots, inside and out. The rounded roots are slightly smaller than most and mild in flavor.

'**Bianca Colleto Viola**,' which translates to "white turnip with a red collar," is from Italy and has excellent flavor. It produces a large, slightly elongated root with red shoulders in mid-season. '**Gold Ball**' is very similar to a rutabaga, with its yellow flesh and smooth, yellow skin. The round roots are 3–4 inches across, have a buttery flavor and are never woody. '**Hinona Kabu**' is an unusual turnip, with elongated roots, 1–2 inches in diameter and 13 inches long. This Japanese variety has purple shoulders, and the greens are as delicious as the root. '**Milan**' is a baby turnip with a buttery flavor, bright red shoulders and white bottoms. '**Milan White**' has a similar flavor but more of a semi-flattened shape and is all white, inside and out. '**Royal Crown**' is an early turnip, bearing globular, smooth-skinned roots with purple shoulders and creamy white bottoms, and deep green leaves. '**Oasis**' can be picked at any size. It bears super sweet roots in 50 days. They can be eaten raw, whole like an apple or grated for salads and snacks. The flavor has been compared to that of a melon.

Problems and Pests

Cabbage root maggots, cabbage worms, cabbage white butterfly larvae, aphids, flea beetles, rust, downy mildew, powdery mildew and clubroot are possible problems.

The rutabaga originated in Europe and has been in cultivation for over 4000 years.

Sorrel

Rumex

Somewhere between salad green and herb, sorrel features tangy, sour leaves equally at home in a salad of mixed greens or in soups, marinades and egg dishes. Sorrel is similar to spinach but tolerates heat more successfully.

Starting

Sow the seed directly in the garden in fall or spring. Set out transplants when available.

Growing

Sorrel grows well in **full sun, light shade** or **partial shade**. The soil should be **fertile, acidic, humus rich, moist** and fairly **well drained.** Mulch to conserve moisture.

Divide sorrel every 3 or 4 years to keep the plant vigorous and the leaves tender and tasty. This plant self-seeds if flowering spikes are not removed.

Harvesting

Pick leaves as needed in spring, early summer or fall. Remove flower spikes as they emerge to prolong the leaf harvest. Once the weather warms

Sorrel that has bolted and gone to flower (above)

up and the plant goes to flower, the leaves lose their pleasant flavor. If you cut the plant back a bit at this point, you will have fresh leaves to harvest in late summer and fall when the weather cools again.

Tips

A tasty and decorative addition to the vegetable, herb or ornamental garden, French sorrel also makes an attractive groundcover and can be included in mixed container plantings.

Recommended

R. acetosa (garden sorrel, broad leaf sorrel) is a vigorous, clump-forming perennial. The inconspicuous flowers are borne on a tall stem that emerges from the center

of the clump. This plant grows 18–36 inches tall and spreads about 12 inches.

R. scutatus (French sorrel, buckler leaf sorrel) forms a low, slow-spreading clump of foliage. Stronger tasting but less plentiful than garden sorrel, the leaves hold their flavor better in warm weather. It grows 6–18 inches tall and spreads up to 24 inches.

Problems and Pests

Sorrel is generally problem free. Snails, slugs, rust and leaf spot can cause problems occasionally.

Oxalic acid gives sorrel leaves their flavor, and though they are safe to eat, in large quantities they can cause stomach upset.

Soybeans

Glycine

Also known as edamame, and popular for years in Asia, Californians have only recently discovered these meaty, tasty, protein-rich vegetables for snacks, salads and more. Simmer seeds in the pod, then pop them out and eat—or shell and then roast the seeds. If you're curious about the taste before you commit to growing them, you can find them shelled and unshelled in the freezer section.

Starting

Sow seeds directly into the garden after the last frost date has passed and the soil has warmed up. Seeds can be planted quite close together when space is at a premium, but ideally, give them 12–18 inches.

Growing

Soybeans grow best in **full sun** but tolerate some light afternoon shade.

The soil should be of **average fertility** and **well drained**. To avoid mildew, make sure they get good air circulation.

Soybeans contain all nine essential amino acids, have no cholesterol and are low in saturated fats and sodium. They are an excellent source of dietary fiber and are high in iron, calcium, B vitamins, zinc, lecithin, phosphorus and magnesium.

Harvesting

Harvest the beans when the pods are plump and full but the seeds are still tender and green. Alternatively, grow pods to maturity and use dry beans in soups and stews.

Tips

Soybeans are very ornamental, with attractive leaves and plentiful flowers. They can be used to make low, temporary hedges or planted in small groups in a border.

Recommended

G. max is a bushy annual that produces clusters of large-seeded pods. There are several available soybean cultivars. Great for snacking, **'Beer Friend'** produces plants 36 inches tall with abundant pods 3 inches long containing 3–4 beans. Heirloom **'Butterbean'** is a bushy plant 24 inches tall with delicious, green seeds ready in 90 days. A great short-season type, **'Envy'** is ready in 75 days but may have lower yields than others. For high yields, try **'Be Sweet,'** which produces about 30 pods per plant and is ready in 85 days. **'Green Pearls'** produces soybeans ready in only 65 days on short, 12-inch-tall bushes.

Problems and Pests

Leaf spot, bacterial blight, rust, bean beetles and aphids can cause problems.

Spinach

Spinacia

Nutritious and versatile, spinach stars in a wide variety of dishes. A cool-season vegetable, spinach goes to seed in warm weather. Consider sorrel as an alternative for warm-weather planting.

Starting

Direct sow spinach in spring as soon as the soil can be worked. In warm-weather areas, sow in fall to take advantage of cooler weather. Space the seeds approximately 8–10 inches apart.

Growing

Spinach grows well in **full sun** or **light shade** and prefers cool weather and a cool location. The soil should be **fertile, moist** and **well drained**. Add a layer of mulch to help keep the soil cool and to delay bolting. Bolt-resistant varieties are also available.

Harvesting

Harvest spinach leaves about 7 weeks after planting. Pick leaves, as needed, a few at a time from each plant. For greater quantities, cut the entire plant

The unrelated New Zealand spinach (Tetragonia expansa) is an excellent and interesting alternative to regular spinach. The leaves can be used in the same way, but the plant is far more heat resistant, upright and branching in habit and can be planted in summer as regular spinach begins to fade. It will grow quickly in the heat of summer and be ready for a late summer and fall harvest.

Smooth-leaved spinach has thin, tender, sweet leaves, while savoy-leaved spinach has broader, thicker, crinkled leaves that hold up better to cooking.

just above where it emerges from the ground—you may get a second crop. Flavor deteriorates as the weather warms and the plant matures and flowers.

Tips

Spinach's dark green foliage is attractive when mass planted and provides a good contrast for brightly colored annual and perennial flowers. Try it in a mixed container kept nearby for convenient harvesting.

Recommended

S. oleracea forms a dense, bushy clump of glossy, dark green, smooth or crinkled (savoyed) foliage.

Spinach beginning to flower and bolt

Plants are ready for harvest in about 45 days. Slow-bolting **'America'** has great flavor and is ideal for spring or fall planting. An All-America Selections winner, savoyed **'Melody Hybrid'** resists disease. Smooth-leaved **'Space'** is a disease-resistant type ready to eat in only 50 days. **'Bloomsdale'** produces dark green, deeply savoyed foliage. Many strains of this cultivar are also available. **'Correnta'** is a smooth-leaved variety with tender, dark green leaves. **'Scarlet'** has attractive dark red veins. **'Tyee'** is a semi-savoy variety that is very bolt resistant. **'Fiorana'** is an early variety, ready for harvest in 25–40 days. This is a great hybrid for successive plantings throughout the growing season. Because it can be harvested at any size, it's great for containers. **'Regal'** is well-suited to dense plantings and is ideal as baby spinach. **'Olympia'** is ready in 46 days, bearing vigorous, dark green leaves that are slow to bolt. With good heat and mildew resistance, **'Unipack 151'** is a slightly later variety, ready in 50 days. It is a semi-savoy spinach with dark green, tender but thick leaves.

Problems and Pests

Avoid powdery and downy mildew by keeping a bit of space between each plant for good airflow.

Squash

Cucurbita

Native to the Americas, squash falls into two categories: summer and winter. The groupings reflect when we eat the squash more than any real difference in the plants themselves. Grown during the warm weather months, summer squash includes thin-skinned varieties such as patty pan and crookneck squash and zucchini. They're harvested when immature and eaten immediately. Winter squash is also started in warm weather, but it's harvested during cool weather. With firmer rinds and thicker skins, winter squash includes pumpkins, butternut squash and acorn squash. These keep longer in storage.

Starting

For a headstart, start seeds in peat pots indoors 6–8 weeks before the last frost date. Keep them in a bright location to minimize stretching. Transplants are commonly available. Plant out or direct sow after the last frost date and once the soil has warmed up. Plant on mounds of soil to ensure there is good drainage away from the base of the plant.

Spacing for seeds or plants will depend on the particular squash. Check the seed packet or plant tag for specifics. Generally, though,

Essential to growing squash successfully is fertilizing with compost tea or liquid fish fertilizer every 2–3 weeks.

squash require a lot of space, roughly 24–36 inches. Squash grows as a vine and non-vining bush. Where space is at a premium, grow vines vertically or choose bush types.

Growing

Squash grows best in **full sun** but tolerates light shade from companion plants. The soil should be **fertile, humus rich, moist** and **well drained**. Mulch well to keep the soil moist. Put straw or mulch under developing fruit of pumpkins and other heavy winter squash to protect the skin while it is tender.

Since both male and female flowers appear on each plant, you might think pollination would be a simple matter of wind-born pollen transfer. Nature evidently had other ideas. The pollen

Don't worry if some of your summer squash are too mature or some of your winter squash are not mature enough. Summer squash can be cured and will keep for a couple of months. They are still useful for muffins and loaves. Immature winter squash can be harvested and used right away; try them stuffed, baked or barbecued.

is sticky and can only be transferred by bees (or very dedicated gardeners). Grow squash near bee-attracting herbs and flowers to increase production.

Zucchini sometimes produces only male flowers when first blooming. This can be frustrating for gardeners who find spent blossoms on the ground—and no fruit on the plant. Don't worry! Soon the plant will start putting out female flowers, and there will be male flowers ready to pollinate them.

Harvesting

Summer squash are tastiest when picked and eaten young. Harvest when they are small: zucchini should be 6–8 inches, patty pan 3–4 inches and crookneck 4–7 inches long. The more you pick, the more the plants will produce. Cut fruit cleanly from

the plant, and avoid damaging the leaves and stems to prevent disease and insect problems.

Harvest winter squash when they are mature. You should be able to press into the skin without leaving an indentation. Harvest winter squash carefully to avoid damaging the skins. Allow them to cure in a warm, dry place for a few weeks until the skins become thick and hard. Store in a cool, dry place and check regularly for spoilage.

Tips

Mound-forming squash, with their tropical-looking leaves, add interest to borders as feature plants. Heavy-fruited trailing types will wind happily through a border of taller plants or shrubs. Train small-fruited trailing selections up trellises. All squash can be grown in containers, but the mound-forming and shorter-trailing selections are usually most attractive; the long-trailing types end up as a stem that leads over the edge of the container.

Recommended

Squash plants are generally similar in appearance, with medium to large leaves held on long stems. Plants are trailing in habit, but some form very short vines, so they appear to be more mound forming. Bright yellow, trumpet-shaped, male and female flowers are borne separately but on the same plant. Female flowers can be distinguished by their short stem and by the juvenile fruit at the base of the flower. Male flowers have longer stems.

Summer squash are available in a variety of shapes and colors, including:

- scallop or patty pan, which are rounded, no bigger than the palm of your hand and have soft skins, often in pale colors, and white flesh

- constricted neck squash, which are thinner at the stem than the blossom end and usually have yellow skin and white flesh; also known as crookneck or straightneck squash, depending on whether the stem is straight or crooked

- cylindrical to club-shaped, which are usually varying shades of green but may be yellow- or white-skinned, with white flesh; also known as Italian marrow.

Winter squash are also available in a variety of types but are not really divided into groups. They do vary greatly in shape, size, texture and color, but they all have hard or thick rinds and thick but tender, often sweet and fibrous flesh.

There are four species of squash commonly grown in gardens. They vary incredibly in appearance and can be smooth or warty, round, elongated or irregular. They can be dark green, tan, creamy white or bright orange, solid, striped or spotted. The size ranges from tiny, round zucchini that would fit in the palm of a child's hand to immense pumpkins that could hold two or three children. Experiment with different types to

'Butternut' (above)

find which ones grow best in your garden and which ones you like best.

C. argyrosperma (*C. mixta*) includes cushaw squash and is not very well known. These plants generally take 100 days or more to mature. Some are grown for their edible seeds, while others are used in baking and are good for muffins, loaves and pies. There aren't a lot of varieties to choose from, but two are definitely worth mentioning. **'Winter Cushaw'** is a very large squash with a crooked neck, green skin with creamy white stripes and speckles, and a slightly sweet, yellow flesh. Heirloom **'Green Striped'** is very disease resistant and can grow up to 20 pounds.

C. maxima includes buttercup squash, hubbard and kabocha. These plants generally need 90–110 days to mature. They keep very well, often longer than any other squash, and have sweet, fine-textured flesh. The list of varieties is endless, but here are a few of the best or most interesting. **'Buttercup'** has a dark green rind with silvery gray lines, and dark yellow flesh that is sweet and nutty and similar to sweet potato in texture. **'Sweet Mama'** is also a buttercup squash, with striped green skin and sweet, yellow flesh. **'Ambercup'** is a kabocha variety with streaked orange skin and orange flesh, and **'Hakkori,'** also a kabocha, has deep green skin and orange, extremely sweet flesh.

C. moschata includes butternut squash and usually needs 95 or more days to mature. These squash keep well and are popular baked or for soups and stews. An endless array

of varieties is readily available, including **'Butternut,'** which bears bottle-shaped, creamy brown fruits with orange-yellow flesh that is nutty in flavor. **'Butternut Supreme'** also has a bulbous base with an elongated neck, tan skin and yellow flesh, but in a bigger size and higher yields. **'Waltham Butternut'** is a late variety with dark yellow flesh, tan skin and a blocky base.

C. pepo is the largest group of squash and includes summer squash, such as zucchini, and many winter squash, such as pumpkins, acorn squash, spaghetti squash, dumpling squash and gourds. Summer squash are ready to harvest in 45–50 days, and the winter squash in this group take from 70–75 days for acorn and spaghetti squash to 95–120 days for some of the larger pumpkins. As the largest and most diverse group, there are countless varieties to choose from.

Examples of summer squash include the following. '**Cocozelle**' is an heirloom bush zucchini with high yields. Smooth, spineless, long-producing '**Dark Star**' is a hybrid-heirloom cross. '**Ambassador**' is an easy to grow, medium green type. Abundant, early '**Greyzini**' is ready in 47 days. '**One Ball**' is an early variety, bearing round, yellow fruits with white flesh, about the size of a billiard ball. '**Eight Ball**' is similar but with green flesh. '**Early Prolific Straightneck**' is a vigorous squash, ready for harvest when the fruits are 4–6 inches long. The flesh is tender and delicious. '**Sunny Delight**' is an early variety of a scallop or mini squash, round, flat and small enough to hold in the palm of your hand. It has bright yellow, thin, edible skin and tender flesh. '**Vegetable Marrow White Bush**' is considered unusual because of its white skin. It resembles a zucchini in shape but is creamy yellow when mature. Try patty pan varieties '**Reve Scallopini**,' with a flattened shape and dark green color, tiny **'Patty Pan,'** and yellow **'Sunburst.'** Productive crooknecks include **'Early Golden Summer'** and **'Yellow Crookneck.'** For containers, try compact crooknecks **'Dixie'** and **'Sundance.'**

The following are some of the most interesting and reliable winter pumpkin selections. Heirloom **'Big Max'** is a huge, round, pinkish orange pumpkin, reaching weights of 100 pounds or more if left to mature in the right environment. **'Freaky Tom'** has a heavily warted, dark orange rind that is great for Halloween carving. **'Jack O'Lantern'** is another pumpkin ideal for carving because of its smooth, firm, bright orange rind. Heirloom **'Sugar Pie'** is wonderful for baked goods, as is **'Small Sugar,'** a super sweet baking squash. **'Rouge Vif d'Etamps'** ('Cinderella') is an heirloom squash. It bears vivid, red-skinned, flattened, heavily ribbed fruits, up to 24 inches across and 15–20 pounds, with moist, orange flesh ideal for pies. For fun decorations, try a miniature pumpkin. **'Jack Be Little'** fruit is only 3–4 inches across and 2 inches tall; the plant can be grown in a large container.

Acorn squash, from the winter grouping, include All-America Selections winner **'Cream of the Crop,'** with white rind and golden flesh, and tasty green hybrid **'Table Ace.'** Rare **'Batwing Acorn,'** ready in 75 days, has an unusual patchy, dark orange and green, rounded, ribbed rind, and **'Honeybear,'** a variety with dark green skin and sweet flesh in a mini form, averages 1 pound each.

Problems and Pests

Problems with mildew, cucumber beetles, stem borers, bacterial wilt and whiteflies can occur. Ants may snack on damaged plants and fruit, and mice will eat and burrow into squash for the seeds in fall.

Sunchokes

Jerusalem Artichokes

Helianthus

An edible tuber of the sunflower family, sunchokes taste like artichokes, radishes or water chestnuts, depending on who is describing the flavor. These tubers were a diet staple for Native Americans and later became popular with European settlers as well. The other common name, Jerusalem artichoke, was thought to have derived from the idea that the sunchokes were food for the "new Jerusalem."

Starting

Sunchokes can be sown directly into the garden in spring around the last frost date. Water well until plants become established. Sunchokes are perennial and will grow back each year as long as you leave some of the tubers in place in fall.

Growing

Sunchokes grow best in **full sun**. The soil should be of **average fertility, humus rich, moist** and **well drained**, though plants adapt to a variety of conditions. They become quite drought tolerant as summer progresses.

If you can't find sunchokes in the nursery, look in the grocery store. Plant chunks that are 1½ inches big with at least one eye. Choose a location where you can enjoy

Sunchokes store energy in the tubers as a carbohydrate called inulin, rather than as starch. They are filling, but the energy is not readily absorbed by the body and does not affect blood sugar levels, making these tubers useful for people with diabetes or who are trying to lose weight.

your sunchokes for many years. They spread by underground runners and are potentially invasive.

Harvesting

Sunchoke tubers are usually ready to harvest in fall. They should be stored in a cool, dry, well-ventilated area. They have only a small trace of starch but contain plenty of inulin, which turns into fructose when they're stored in a cold room, refrigerator or the ground. In fact, once the tubers are cooled in storage, they develop a much sweeter taste.

Tips

Sunchokes are crunchier and sweeter than potatoes, with a hint of artichoke. They can be boiled, baked, fried, steamed, stewed or eaten raw. They cook more quickly than potatoes and become mushy if overcooked. Tubers are generally knobby; varieties without knobs are easier to clean and cook.

Recommended

H. tuberosus is a tall, bushy, tuberous perennial. It grows 6–10 feet tall and spreads 2–4 feet. Bright yellow flowers are produced in late summer and fall. There are a great many sunchokes to choose from, but here are some of the ones that stand out. **'Sun Choke'** is grown mainly in California and tastes great raw or cooked. **'Mulles Rose'** produces large, white tubers with rose-purple eyes. **'Stampede'** is an early yielding, large sunchoke, ready in 90 days with white flesh. **'Fuseau'** is a long, straight tuber, knob-free with white flesh. **'Sugarball'** originated in Hungary and is super sweet. **'Sakhalinski Rouge'** produces branching, smooth tubers flushed with violet and with fewer knobs. **'Boston Red'** has large, knobby, rosy red tubers with smooth outer skin. **'Dwarf Sunray'** bears tender, crisp tubers that do not require peeling. **'Golden Nugget'** has golden tubers that resemble carrots, tapered at the tips. **'Jack's Copperclad'** is an heirloom variety and is difficult to find, but well worth the search. It bears plump, knobby tubers with dark copper or rose-purple skin and sweet flesh.

Problems and Pests

Sunchokes are generally problem free.

Sweet Potatoes

Ipomoea

Surprisingly, a sweet potato is not really a potato but rather a tropical vine related to morning glory. But that's not where the confusion ends. Sweet potatoes and yams are referred to interchangeably, but they're actually quite different. The sweet potato, *Ipomoea batatas*, has moist, sweet, orange-red flesh, while the yam, *Dioscorea* species, has dry, starchy, yellowish white, potato-like flesh. The sweet potato has a much wider appeal to gardeners and chefs alike because of its versatility and delicious flavor. Sweet potatoes need consistent warmth above 50° F and do not do well in northern California.

Starting

Growing sweet potatoes is a long process involving multiple steps and many months.

Sweet potatoes are grown from slips, or rooted cuttings. Purchase slips from

Lift the tubers from the soil once the vines begin to yellow or when they're still slightly immature. Use the tubers fresh from the garden or store them in a cool, dark location for up to a week, unless you're curing them for the long haul.

a garden center, local farm, mail-order company or online vegetable supplier. Once you've grown a crop of sweet potatoes, you can also overwinter the roots for the next year's crop. Don't bother trying to grow slips from sweet potatoes bought at the grocery store because they are treated to prevent sprouting.

Place slips so that only tips and leaves are showing. Space them 12 inches apart in rows 36 inches apart with ditches between them for improved drainage.

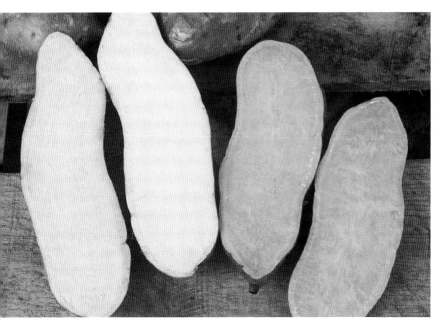

Growing

Sweet potatoes require **full sun** and **moist, sandy** soil. For added heat concentration, cover with black plastic. Cut holes for the foliage and for periodic irrigation. Do not grow sweet potatoes in the same place 2 years in a row to avoid spreading disease.

Harvesting

Sweet potatoes can be harvested as soon as they are large enough to use, usually 110–120 days after planting. For the best flavor, wait until the foliage, or top portion of the plants, starts to turn yellow. Once this has taken place, harvest the roots immediately. Remove the tubers carefully with a garden fork so you don't bruise them. Bruised tubers should be used first, while the rest can be stored for long periods.

If you're going to store them, they should be cured first. Let them sit in the sun for a day, separated and dry, then place them in a humid location out of direct sunlight for roughly 2 weeks. Once the curing stage is complete, store the tubers in a dry, cool location for up to 5 months.

Tips

Sweet potatoes are really a vegetable garden kind of plant and should be planted in a hot and sunny location where they have plenty of space to grow on their own.

Recommended

I. batatas (sweet potato, yam) is a trailing perennial that produces deeply lobed, deep green leaves, funnel-shaped, violet flowers and tuberous roots with orange flesh and skin. Suggested varieties include '**Centennial**,' which is ready as a baby baking sweet potato in only 90 days, with heavy yields and good storage. '**Jewel**' is a heavy producer of moist tubers with light orange flesh. Vigorous '**Garnet**' sports purplish red skin with orange flesh. '**Ruddy**' is a reddish-skinned variety that is more pest resistant than the popular '**Beauregard**.'

Problems and Pests

Sweet potatoes are rarely bothered by diseases, but might experience problems with nematodes, aphids, flea beetles, leaf hoppers and wireworms.

Tomatoes

Lycopersicon

Californians love their tomatoes. It's a rare garden that doesn't have at least one, and most gardens have multiple kinds—no surprise in a state that grows in excess of 500 varieties. With the rising interest in heirlooms, gardeners have embraced unusual yellow, pink, striped and nearly black tomatoes in sizes large and small with odd and traditional shapes. On many spring and summer weekends, you can find local tomato tastings offered by expert growers. Even gardeners who lack the ideal hot and sunny conditions favored by most tomatoes have now discovered that they *can* grow them if they choose the right kinds for their climate.

'Roma' (above)

Starting

Tomatoes can be started from seed indoors 6–8 weeks before the last frost date. An increasing number of heirloom and hybrid plants are available from nurseries and garden centers.

Plant seedlings and transplants deeply. Roots form along the buried stem, producing extra growing power and support. Bury the stem to the lowest set of leaves, or as close to the first set as possible. Trim off leaves that touch soil to reduce the possibility of disease.

Spacing varies for the different selections, so check the seed packet or plant tag for specifics. Tomatoes need good air circulation; don't crowd them.

When tomato plants were first introduced to Europe, they were grown as ornamentals, not for their edible fruit.

Growing

Tomatoes, particularly big-fruited types, grow best in **full sun**. Smaller cherry and grape varieties can get by with a little less. The soil should be **average to fertile, humus rich, moist** and **well drained**. Keep tomatoes evenly moist to encourage good fruit production. Overwatering, however, yields less flavorful tomatoes. Stick a finger in the soil and water only when it feels dry an inch below the surface. To reduce disease, keep foliage dry and don't water late in the day.

If flowers form but fall off without fruiting, make your tomato patch more attractive to pollinators. Plant sweet alyssum and other bee-attractors nearby. Blossom drop can also occur if temperatures are too high (above 85° F) during the day or too high or low (70° F or above, 55° F or below) at night.

Except for very small bush selections, tomatoes tend to be quite tall and are prone to flopping unless stakes, wire hoops, tomato cages or other supports are used.

Harvesting

Pick the fruit as soon as it is ripe. Tomatoes pull easily from the vine with a gentle twist when they are ready for picking.

Tips

Tomatoes may be tall and vining, short and bushy and everything in between. They have both attractive little flower clusters and vibrantly colored fruit. Many selections grow well in containers and can be included in patio gardens and hanging baskets, particularly determinate (bush) varieties.

Always grow at least one cherry tomato. They fruit reliably, abundantly and quickly. Larger varieties need more time to develop and so sometimes fall prey to pests and diseases.

Recommended

L. lycopersicum includes bushy or vine-forming annuals with pungent, bristly leaves and stems. Determinate (or bush) plants grow to 3–5 feet tall and bear all their fruit within 4–6 weeks; they seldom need staking. Indeterminate plants continue to grow until killed by disease or frost. Clusters of yellow flowers are followed by fruit from midsummer through the first frost. Fruits ripen to red, orange, pink or yellow and come in many shapes and sizes. Beefsteak tomatoes are the largest; currant are the smallest. Tomato fruit size and plant size do not always match; many cherry tomatoes are born on tall, rangy vines. Some do well in all areas of the state; others do well only in certain areas. Even cooler regions can grow tomatoes if they are short-season types. Browse through seed

catalogs and discover the many available offerings. Try a few new ones each year to find your favorites.

When shopping, look for the initials AVF-NTSt. They indicate disease resistance to the following: **A**lternaria stem canker, *Verticillium* wilt, *Fusarium* wilt, **N**ematodes, **T**obacco mosaic virus and **St**emphylium gray spot. Most heirlooms do not resist these diseases. Look for new organic sprays that provide protection.

The University of California Division of Agriculture and Natural Resources divides the state into three climatic tomato growing zones:

- Zone A: coastal areas from Santa Barbara south; coastal foothills and mountain ranges from San Diego through Marin counties; foothills surrounding

Tomatoes growing within the confines of a tomato cage for support (above)

the Central, Napa and Sonoma valleys; the cities of Santa Barbara, Los Angeles, Santa Ana and San Diego; and other areas where summer temperatures are usually below 95° F.

- Zone B: inland valleys and high and low deserts; the Central, Sacramento, San Gabriel and San Fernando valleys; interior valleys of San Diego county; the cities of Redding, Sacramento, Fresno, Bakersfield, Pomona, Riverside and El Cajon; and other inland growing areas where daytime temperatures regularly exceed 95° F.

- Zone C: intermediate central and northern coastal areas; cool coastal areas from Santa Maria north to the Oregon border; the San Francisco Peninsula and areas with direct exposure to the San Francisco Bay; northern coastal foothills; most mountains and mountain valley regions; the cities of Santa Maria, Monterey, Santa Cruz, San Jose, San Francisco, Oakland and Eureka; and other areas with cool summers with evening temperatures in the 45–55° F range.

Consider the following tomatoes for Zone A. Tangy **'Black Plum'** is a Russian type with abundant 2-inch, mahogany red globes.

One of the darkest of the black tomatoes, taste-test winner **'Carbon'** also gets high marks for productivity. Versatile French **'Carmello'** is one of the most productive tomatoes and tastes equally fine cooked or raw. **'Dr. Carolyn'** is an unusual light yellow, flavorful cherry variety that looks lovely mixed with red tomatoes. From China, sweet **'Golden Gem'** bears abundant crack-resistant cherry tomatoes. Sweet red cherry **'Isis Candy'** gets top marks in taste tests and resists cracking, too. Hardy pink **'Julia Child'** bears 4-inch beefsteak tomatoes. **'Lemon Boy'** is a beautiful bright yellow, disease-resistant hybrid that bears 8-ounce fruit. One of the most popular tomatoes in Japan, pink, medium-sized

'**Momotaro**' is taking California by storm with its balanced sweet/acid flavor.

If you're in Zone B, try '**Better Boy**,' a flavorful, disease-resistant hybrid that yields big, 10-ounce fruit. Hardy heirloom '**Husky**' bears red, 7-ounce tomatoes. '**Kellogg's Breakfast**' is from West Virginia and bears golden, 1-pound fruit with a distinctive tangy flavor. Looking for a paste tomato? Try '**Super Marzano**,' which holds up well in cooking. '**Sweet 100**' is another popular cherry. It lives up to its name in taste and productivity.

For Zone C, Russian heirloom '**Alaska**' is a semi-determinate that produces abundant red, salad-size tomatoes. From the same area of the world, large heirloom '**Anna Russian**' yields 1-pound, oxheart-shaped, red fruit. The charmingly named '**Black Prince**,' a favorite black variety from Siberia, yields 2-inch fruit with complex flavor. '**Glacier**' starts producing flowers when it is only 4 inches tall and goes on to produce many 2- to 3-ounce, red fruits. Hailing from Siberia, '**Paul Robeson**' churns out 4-inch, rich, flavorful, dark fruit. Large heirloom '**San Francisco Fog**' withstands overcast weather and yields lots of 2- to 3-inch, red fruit. From Oregon, popular '**Siletz**' has 8- to 10-ounce, nicely flavored, red fruit. '**Stupice**' is a taste-test winner for its delicious combo of sweetness and acidity in 2- to 3-ounce, red fruit.

The unusual color of '**White Cherry**' makes it stand out in the salad bowl.

Many perform well in two zones. '**Ace 55**' is a dependable, low-acid tomato that produces 12- to 14-ounce, red fruit (Zones A, B). Vigorous, rangy, full-flavor '**Black Cherry**' resists disease (Zones B, C). Hybrid '**Early Girl**' may not sound as exciting as some of the heirlooms, yet it beat them in a blind taste test (Zones A, B). Extra-early, compact, pink '**Early Wonder**' is a proven producer (Zones B, C). A bush variety with 1-inch fruit, '**Green Grape**' tastes great and looks good on the plate (Zones A, B). With an unusual lemon-lime flavor, the 2-inch fruit of '**Green Zebra**' has distinctive green-striped gold coloring (Zones A, B).

The following varieties do well throughout California. For cherry tomatoes, '**Sungold**' is an early ripener with a heavy crop; '**Super Sweet 100 Hybrid VF**' has reliable red fruit clusters; and '**Yellow Pear**' has low-acid, mild, pear-shaped fruit. Selections suited for containers include '**Better Bush Hybrid VFN**,' an early ripening determinate type; '**Patio Hybrid VASt**,' which is extremely compact; '**Small Fry VFNASt**,' an All-America Selections winner; and '**Toy Boy VF**,' a very early type. Good standard selections include large, intermediate '**Champion Hybrid VFNT**' and abundant '**Early Pick Hybrid VF**.'

Problems and Pests

Problems with tobacco mosaic virus, aphids, fungal wilt, blossom end rot and nematodes can occur.

Tomato horn worms can ruin a tomato quickly; watch for droppings because the large worms camouflage themselves and are hard to spot.

Tomatillos (Physalis ixocarpa) *are related to tomatoes, and the plants have similar cultural requirements. The fruit is encased in a delicate papery husk. They are ready to pick when the husk is loose and the fruit has turned from green to gold or light brown.*

Basil

Ocimum

The sweet, fragrant leaves of basil add a delicious, licorice-like flavor to salads and tomato-based dishes.

Starting

Basil is easy to start from seed. Start indoors about 4 weeks before the last frost date, or sow directly in sun-warmed soil once the danger of frost has passed. Press seeds into soil, then gently sift a little more soil over them. Keep soil moist. Seeds will germinate in about a week. Look for container-grown plants in midsummer.

Growing

Basil grows best in a warm, sheltered location in **full sun**. The soil should be **fertile, moist** and **well drained**. Pinch the flowering tips regularly to encourage bushy growth and leaf production. Mulch soil to retain water and to keep weeds down.

Harvesting

Pluck leaves or pinch back stem tips as needed. Basil is tastiest if used fresh, but it can be dried or frozen.

Tips

Although basil grows best in a warm spot outdoors, it can be grown successfully indoors in a pot by a bright window, providing you with fresh leaves all year. Some of the purple-leaved varieties are very decorative and make fine borders.

Recommended

O. basilicum is one of the most popular culinary herbs. There are dozens of varieties, including ones with large or tiny, green or purple, smooth or ruffled leaves, as well as varied flavors including anise, cinnamon and lemon. **'Green Globe'** forms a rounded mound of tiny leaves. **'Mammoth'** has huge leaves, up to 10 inches long and about half as wide. **'Purple Ruffles'** has dark purple leaves with frilly margins. **'Siam Queen'** is a cultivar of Thai basil with dark green foliage and dark purple flowers and stems. Try **'Scented Trio'** from Renee's Garden, a three-pack of seeds including **'Cinnamon'** basil, **'Mrs. Burns'** citrus-scented lemon basil and garnet-colored **'Red Rubin'** basil.

Problems and Pests

Fusarium wilt may afflict basil. Keep caterpillars from chomping on it by using B.t.k.

Features: bushy annual with fragrant, decorative, edible leaves; white or light purple flowers **Height:** 12–24" **Spread:** 12–18"

Borage

Borago

Both the leaves and flowers of borage are edible, making an interesting addition to salads. They have a very light, cucumber-like flavor. The flowers can also be frozen in ice cubes or used to decorate cakes and other desserts.

Starting

Sow seed directly in the garden in spring. This plant resents transplanting thanks to a long taproot but recovers fairly quickly if moved when young.

Growing

Borage grows well in **full sun** or **partial shade**. It likes **average, light, well-drained** soil but will adapt to most conditions; it's a good drought-tolerant choice. Borage is a vigorous self-seeder.

Harvesting

Pick borage leaves when they are young and fuzzy because they become bristly as they mature. Pick flowers any time after they open; they tend to change color from blue to pinkish mauve as they mature.

Tips

Borage makes an attractive addition to herb and vegetable gardens, as well as to flower beds and borders. The plant should be pinched back when young to encourage bushy growth; otherwise, it tends to flop over and develop a sprawling habit.

Recommended

B. officinalis is a bushy plant with bristly leaves and stems. It bears clusters of star-shaped, blue or purple flowers from midsummer to fall. A white-flowered variety is available.

Problems and Pests

Rare outbreaks of powdery mildew and aphids are possible but don't seem to be detrimental to the plant.

Borage attracts bees, butterflies and other pollinators and beneficial insects to the garden.

Features: bushy, bristly annual herb; edible, bristly leaves; edible, blue, purple or white, summer flowers **Height:** 18–28" **Spread:** 18–24"

Chives

Allium

The delicate onion flavor of chives is best enjoyed fresh. Mix chives into dips, or sprinkle them on salads and baked potatoes. The blooms are striking in the garden and in salads and herbal vinegars.

Starting

Chives can be started indoors 4–6 weeks before the last frost date or planted directly in the garden. They also can be purchased as plants.

Growing

Chives grow well in **full sun** or **partial shade**. The soil should be **fertile, moist** and **well drained**, but chives adapt to most soil conditions. Plants self-seed freely in good growing conditions. The youngest leaves are the most tender and flavorful, so cut plants back to encourage new growth if flavor diminishes over summer.

Harvesting

Chives can be snipped off with scissors all spring, summer and fall, as needed. Flowers are usually used just after they open, and the individual flowers in the cluster are broken apart for use.

Tips

Include decorative chives in a mixed or herbaceous border and let them naturalize. In an herb garden, give them plenty of space for self-seeding.

Recommended

A. schoenoprasum (chives) forms a clump of bright green, cylindrical leaves. Clusters of pinkish purple flowers are produced in early and midsummer. Varieties with white or pink flowers are also available.

A. tuberosum (garlic chives) forms a clump of long, narrow, flat, dark green leaves. Clusters of white flowers are borne all summer. The young leaves have a distinctive garlic flavor. They self-seed more readily than other types.

Problems and Pests

Chives rarely have any problems.

Chives are said to increase appetite and encourage good digestion.

Features: edible foliage; habit; mauve, pink or white flowers **Height:** 8–24"
Spread: 12" or more

Coriander & Cilantro

Coriandrum

This Mediterranean native is a multi-purpose herb. The leaves, called cilantro, are used in salads, salsas and soups. The seeds, called coriander, are used in cakes, pies, chutneys, stews and marmalades. The flavor of each part is quite distinct.

Starting

Coriander can be started from seed 4–6 weeks before the last frost date or sown directly in the garden. Started plants can also be purchased from nurseries, garden centers or herb specialists. Several small sowings two weeks apart will ensure a steady supply of leaves.

Growing

Coriander prefers **full sun** but benefits from afternoon shade during the heat of summer. Too much heat may cause bolting. The soil should be **fertile, light** and **well drained**. This plant dislikes humid conditions and does best during a dry summer.

Harvesting

Harvest leaves as needed throughout summer. Seeds can be harvested as they ripen in fall. Spread out a large sheet and shake the seed heads over it to collect the seeds.

Coriander is one of the best plants for attracting predatory insects to your garden.

Features: airy, delicate habit; edible, fernlike foliage; flat, pinkish white, summer flowers
Height: 18–24" **Spread:** 8–18"

Tips

Coriander has pungent leaves that release their scent as people brush past. The plant is a delight to behold when in flower. Add a plant here and there throughout your borders, both for the visual appeal and to attract beneficial insects.

Recommended

C. sativum is an annual herb that forms a clump of lacy basal foliage. Large, loose clusters of tiny, pinkish white flowers rise above. The seeds ripen in late summer and fall.

Problems and Pests

This plant rarely suffers from any problems.

Dill

Anethum

Dill is majestic and beautiful in any garden setting. If you're growing cucumbers, grow some dill as well because the leaves and seeds are essential for pickling.

Starting

Dill can be sown directly into the garden around the last frost date. Make several small sowings every couple of weeks to ensure a steady supply of leaves.

Growing

Dill grows best in **full sun** in a sheltered location out of strong winds. The soil should be of **poor to average fertility, moist** and **well drained**. Sow seeds in place. Don't grow dill near fennel because the two plants will cross-pollinate, and the seeds of both plants will lose their distinct flavors.

Harvesting

Pick the leaves as needed throughout summer and dry for use in winter. Harvest the seeds by shaking the seed heads over a sheet once they ripen in late summer or fall.

Tips

With its feathery leaves, dill is an attractive addition to a mixed bed or border. Include it in a vegetable garden or any sunny location. Dill also attracts butterflies and beneficial insects to the garden.

Recommended

A. graveolens is an annual herb that forms a clump of feathery foliage. Clusters of yellow flowers are borne at the tops of sturdy stems.

Problems and Pests

Dill rarely suffers from any problems.

Features: feathery, edible foliage; yellow, summer flowers; edible seeds Height: 2–5' Spread: 12" or more

Garlic

Allium

Garlic is not the most ornamental plant, but the light green leaves make a good groundcover and repel several common garden pests.

Starting

Garlic is generally grown from sets (cloves) that can be started in fall or spring. Also, try planting cloves from the grocery store. Plant pointed end up. Where winters are mild, plant in fall for a spring crop.

Growing

Garlic grows best in **full sun**. The soil should be **fertile, moist** and **well drained**. Although the flowers are quite attractive and often intriguing, they should be removed so the plant devotes all its energy to producing bulbs rather than seeds.

Harvesting

This plant can be dug up in fall once the leaves have yellowed and died back. Lift gently with a garden fork to avoid cracking the bulbs.

Features: perennial bulb; narrow, strap-like leaves; white, summer flowers **Height:** 6–24"
Spread: 8"

Softneck garlic can be stored for a longer time than hardneck varieties, but it is not as hardy.

Tips

Garlic takes up little space and can be tucked into any spare spot in your garden.

Recommended

A. sativum var. *ophioscordon* (hardneck garlic) has a stiff central stem around which the cloves develop.

A. sativum var. *sativum* (softneck garlic) develops more cloves but has no stiff stem. The soft leaves are often used to braid garlic bulbs together for storage.

Problems and Pests

A few rot problems can occur, but this plant is generally trouble free.

Nasturtiums

Tropaeolum

These fast-growing, brightly colored flowers are easy to grow, making them popular with beginners and experienced gardeners alike. From South America, nasturtiums have a peppery flavor.

Starting

Direct sow seed once the danger of frost has passed. Where winters are warm, sow in fall for blooms in winter and spring.

Growing

Nasturtiums prefer **full sun** but tolerate some shade. The soil should be of **poor to average fertility, light, moist** and **well drained**. Rich, over-fertilized soil results in lots of leaves but very few flowers. Let soil drain completely between waterings.

Harvesting

Pick leaves and flowers for fresh use as needed.

Tips

Nasturtiums are used in beds, borders, containers and hanging baskets and on

sloped banks. Grow climbing varieties up trellises, over rock walls or around places that you want to conceal. These problem-solvers thrive in poor locations where other plants refuse to grow and quickly camouflage hard-to-mow slopes.

Recommended

T. majus has a trailing habit, but many cultivars have bushier, more refined habits. Cultivars offer differing flower colors or variegated foliage.

Problems and Pests

These plants rarely suffer from any problems.

Features: bushy or trailing annual; attractive, edible foliage; red, orange, yellow, burgundy, pink, cream, gold, white or bicolored, edible flowers **Height:** 12–18" for dwarf varieties; up to 10' for trailing varieties **Spread:** equal to height

Oregano & Marjoram

Origanum

Relatives of mint, oregano and marjoram are two of the best-known and most frequently used herbs. They are popular in stuffings, soups and stews, and no pizza is complete until sprinkled with fresh or dried oregano. Oregano also complements the delicious Mediterranean stew ratatouille, made from fresh tomatoes, eggplant and zucchini.

Starting

Start oregano and marjoram from seed 4–6 weeks before planting in the garden, or purchase seedlings.

Growing

Oregano and marjoram grow best in **full sun**. The soil should be **average to fertile, neutral to alkaline** and **well drained**. They are somewhat drought tolerant once established, and keeping them on the dry side concentrates flavor. New wood is most productive, so cut plants back in winter or spring. Oregano may self-seed.

Harvesting

Pick leaves as needed and use immediately or dry for later use.

Tips

These bushy perennials make lovely additions to any border and can be trimmed to form low hedges. The flowers attract pollinators and beneficial insects to the garden.

Features: fragrant, edible foliage; white or pink, summer flowers **Height:** 12–32"
Spread: 8–18"

Recommended

O. majorana (marjoram) is upright and shrubby. It has fuzzy, light green leaves and bears white or pink flowers in summer. Where it is not hardy, it can be grown as an annual.

O. vulgare **var.** *hirtum* (oregano, Greek oregano) is the most flavorful culinary variety of oregano. This low, bushy plant has fuzzy, gray-green leaves and bears white flowers. Many other interesting varieties of *O. vulgare* are available, including those with golden, variegated or curly leaves.

Problems and Pests

Problems with oregano and marjoram are rare.

Parsley

Petroselinum

Parsley is far more than an attractive garnish. Flavorful and packed with vitamins, it brightens the flavor of many dishes. Try it as a lovely and useful addition to a container planting.

Starting

Parsley can be sown directly in the garden once the last frost date has passed. Soaking the seeds for 24 hours improves germination. Transplants are also readily available.

Growing

Parsley grows well in **full sun** or **partial shade**. The soil should be **average to fertile, humus rich, moist** and **well drained**.

Harvesting

Pinch parsley to encourage bushy growth. Cut back regularly if you need a large quantity in a recipe, and it will sprout new growth.

Tips

Keep containers of parsley close to the house for easy picking. The bright green leaves and compact habit make parsley a good edging plant for beds and borders. A nutritious addition to a variety of dishes, parsley contains vitamins A and C as well as iron.

Recommended

P. crispum forms a clump of bright green, divided leaves. This biennial is usually grown as an annual. Cultivars may have flat or curly leaves. Flat leaves are tastier, and curly ones are more decorative. Dwarf cultivars are also available.

Problems and Pests

Parsley rarely suffers from any problems.

Features: biennial grown as an annual; bushy habit; attractive, edible foliage
Height: 8–24" **Spread:** 12–24"

Rosemary

Rosmarinus

The needle-like leaves of this fragrant shrub are used to flavor a wide variety of foods, including chicken, pork, lamb, rice, tomato and egg dishes. A little fresh rosemary sprinkled on roasted vegetables is truly delicious. A Mediterranean native, this versatile herb performs well under a variety of conditions and has great value as a landscape plant.

Starting

Specific varieties can be purchased from garden centers, nurseries and specialty growers. Start any time.

Growing

Rosemary prefers **full sun** but tolerates partial shade. The soil should be of **poor to average fertility** and **well drained**. Rosemary thrives on a bit of neglect; be stingy with water and fertilizer. In cold areas, shelter from winter winds. Rosemary takes well to frequent, light pruning.

Harvesting

Pick leaves as needed for use in cooking.

Tips

Grow rosemary as a fragrant hedge that doubles as a convenient source of fresh herbs. Rosemary attracts birds, butterflies and bees.

Recommended

R. officinalis is a dense, bushy, evergreen shrub with narrow, dark green leaves. The habit varies between cultivars from strongly upright to prostrate and spreading. Upright varieties are cold resistant. Flowers are usually shades of blue, but pink-flowered cultivars are available. Varieties include hardy **'Arp,'** 4 feet wide and tall; **'Blue Spires,'** a 6-foot-tall specimen ideal for hedges; **'Huntington Carpet,'** which spreads 18 inches and is useful for covering banks and large areas; and famous **'Tuscan Blue,'** with violet blue flowers and a height of 6–7 feet.

Problems and Pests

Rosemary has few problems.

Features: fragrant, edible, evergreen foliage; bright blue, sometimes pink flowers
Height: 8"–6' **Spread:** 1–4'

Sage

Salvia

A Mediterranean herb, sage is perhaps best known as a flavoring for stuffing. The leaves are also used in soups, stews, sausages and dumplings.

Starting

Start indoors in late winter or early spring, or purchase seedlings.

Growing

Sage does well in **full sun** but prefers **light shade** in the hottest areas. The soil should be of **average fertility** and **well drained**. This plant benefits from a light mulch of compost each year. Sage is drought tolerant once established.

Harvesting

Pick fresh leaves as needed, or dry and freeze them for later use.

Tips

Sage is a good border plant, adding volume to the middle and attractiveness to the front. Sage can also be grown in mixed planters.

Recommended

S. officinalis is a woody, mound-forming perennial with soft, gray-green leaves. Spikes of light purple or blue flowers appear in early and midsummer. Many cultivars with attractive foliage are available, including the yellow-leaved **'Golden Sage,'** the yellow-margined **'Icterina,'** the purple-leaved **'Purpurea'** and the purple, green and cream variegated **'Tricolor,'** which also has a pink flush to the new growth. **'Compacta'** is a small version perfect for containers.

Problems and Pests

Sage rarely suffers from any problems, but it can rot in wet soil.

Features: shrubby perennial with fragrant, decorative, edible foliage; red, white, pink, blue or purple, summer flowers
Height: 12–36" **Spread:** 18–36"

Thyme

Thymus

A member of the mint family, this popular Mediterranean herb is used in soups, stews, casseroles and roasts. Place it where passersby can brush against it to release the pleasant fragrance.

Starting

Common thyme can be started indoors from seed 4–6 weeks before you plan to plant it outdoors. Purchase seedlings at nurseries and garden centers and from specialty growers.

Growing

Thyme does well in **full sun** or **partial shade** in warmer areas. The soil should be **neutral to alkaline** and of **poor to average fertility**. Good drainage is essential. Thyme tolerates drought once established.

Harvesting

Pick leaves as needed or dry for later use.

Tips

Thyme is useful for sunny, dry locations at the front of borders, between or beside paving stones, on rock walls and in containers. Once the plant has finished flowering, shear it back by about half to encourage new growth and to prevent it from becoming too woody.

Features: shrubby perennial with bushy habit; fragrant, decorative, edible foliage; purple, pink or white, summer flowers
Height: 8–16" **Spread:** 8–24"

Recommended

T. × citriodorus (lemon thyme) forms a mound of lemon-scented, dark green foliage. The summer flowers are pale pink. Cultivars with silver- or gold-margined leaves are available.

T. vulgaris (common thyme) forms a bushy mound of fragrant, dark green leaves. The summer flowers may be purple, pink or white. Cultivars with variegated leaves are available.

Problems and Pests

Thyme rarely suffers from any problems, but its roots can rot in poorly drained, wet soils.

When blooming, thyme is a bee magnet. Pleasantly herbal thyme honey goes very well with biscuits.

Appendix: Companion Plants

The following plants, arranged in alphabetical order by common name, all provide certain benefits to other plants when growing in proximity to each other, and/or to the garden in general.

Alliums (*Allium* spp.): group includes onions, garlic, leeks, shallots, chives and others; repel and distract slugs, aphids, carrot flies and cabbage worms

Asters (*Aster* spp.): general insect repellents

Borage (*Borago officinalis*): deters tomato worms; companion to tomatoes, squash and strawberries, improving growth and flavor

Calendula (*Calendula officinalis*): repels and distracts nematodes, beet leaf hoppers and other pests

Caraway (*Carum carvi*): loosens soil where it grows; attracts parasitic wasps and parasitic bees

Carrot (*Daucus carota*): attracts assassin bugs, lacewings, parasitic wasps, yellow jackets and other predatory wasps

Chamomile (*Chamaemelum nobile*): encourages other plants such as herbs, including lavender and rosemary, to increase their essential oil content

Chrysanthemums (*Chrysanthemum* spp.): reduce the number of nematodes

Cilantro/Coriander (*Coriandrum sativum*): scent repels aphids, attracts tachinid flies

Dill (*Anethum graveolens*): attracts hoverflies, wasps, tomato horn worms, honeybees, ichneumonid wasps, aphids, spider mites, squash bugs and cabbage looper

Fennel (*Foeniculum vulgare*): attracts ladybugs, syrphid flies and tachinid flies; repels and distracts aphids

Flax (*Linum usitatissimum*): deters potato bugs; companion to carrots and potatoes, improving growth and flavor

Geraniums (*Pelargonium* spp.): can be attractive to caterpillars, luring them away from adjacent plants

Horseradish (*Armoracia rusticana*): planted at corners of potato patch, will discourage potato bugs

Hyssop (*Hyssopus officinalis*): attracts honeybees and butterflies; repels and distracts cabbage moth larvae and cabbage butterflies

Larkspur (*Consolida ajacis*): protects vines against vine beetles

Lavenders (*Lavandula* spp.): general insect repellents; attract pollinating insects; provide protection against borers and mosquitoes

Lavender cotton (*Santolina chamaecyparissus*): general insect repellent

Lovage (*Levisticum officinale*): attracts ichneumonid wasps and ground beetles

Marigolds (*Tagetes* spp.): discourage beetles, nematodes and other pests

Mints (*Mentha* spp.): improve the flavor and growth of cabbage and tomatoes; deter white cabbage moths

Nasturtium (*Tropaeolum majus*): attracts predatory insects; repels and distracts cabbage loopers, squash bugs, white flies and cucumber beetles

Oregano (*Origanum vulgare*): repels and distracts aphids

Parsley (*Petroselinum crispum*): scent deters carrot flies

Peppers, hot (*Capsicum* spp.): produce a chemical that prevents root rot

Petunia (*Petunia* x *hybrida*): deters and distracts leafhoppers, Japanese beetles, aphids and asparagus beetles

Rue (*Ruta graveolens*): deters beetles in roses and raspberries; do not plant near cabbages, basil or sage

Sage (*Salvia officinalis*): deters cabbage moths and carrot flies

Tansy (*Tanacetum vulgare*): companion to roses and raspberries; deters flying insects, Japanese beetles, striped cucumber beetles, ants and squash bugs

Tomato (*Solanum lycopersicum*): when planted near asparagus, deters asparagus beetles

White alyssum (*Lobularia maritime*): reseeds frequently; helps to break up the soil, adding to organic content

Yarrow (*Achillea millefolium*): attracts predatory wasps, ladybugs, hoverflies and damselbugs

COMPANION PLANT RELATIONSHIPS

Plant	Compatible Plants	Incompatible Plants
apricots	basil, tansy	
asparagus	basil, parsley, tomatoes	
beans	most herbs and vegetables	beets, cabbage, garlic, kohlrabi, onions
beets	broccoli, cabbage, chard, garlic, kohlrabi, onions	beans
broccoli	beans, beets, celery, chamomile, cucumbers, lettuce, mint, onions, oregano, potatoes, thyme, rosemary	
cabbage	Alliums, aromatic herbs, beets, celery, chamomile, chard, spinach, potatoes	beans, corn, dill, parsnips, strawberries, tomatoes
carrots	Alliums, bell peppers, grapes, lettuce, peas, sage, tomatoes	dill, parsnips
cauliflower	beans, celery	strawberries
celery	beans, broccoli, cabbage, cauliflower, leeks, nasturtiums, onions, spinach, tomatoes	parsnips

Plant	Compatible Plants	Incompatible Plants
chard, Swiss	beets, cabbage, lavender, onions	
corn	beans, cucumbers, melons, peas, potatoes, squash, tomatoes	cabbage
cucumbers	beans, broccoli, corn, lettuce, peas, sunflowers, radishes	aromatic herbs, potatoes
eggplant	beans, potatoes, spinach	
garlic	beets, lettuce, chamomile, parsnips, peaches, strawberries, tomatoes	beans, peas
grapes	basil, beans, carrots, geraniums, hyssop, peas	
kohlrabi	beets, onions	beans, tomatoes
leeks	carrots, celery, onions	
lettuce	broccoli, carrots, cucumbers, garlic, onions, radishes, strawberries	
melons	corn, radishes	
onions	beets, bell peppers, broccoli, cabbage, carrots, celery, chamomile, chard, kohlrabi, leeks, lettuce, tomatoes, strawberries	beans, peas
parsley	asparagus, tomatoes	
parsnips	beans, bell peppers, garlic, peas, potatoes, radishes	cabbage, carrots, celery
peaches	garlic, tansy	
peas	most herbs and vegetables	garlic, onions, potatoes
peppers, bell	carrots, onions, parsnips, tomatoes	
potatoes	beans, broccoli, cabbage, corn, eggplant, horseradish, marigolds, parsnips	cucumbers, peas, squash, sunflowers, tomatoes, turnips
radishes	cucumbers, lettuce, melons, nasturtiums, parsnips, peas	hyssop
spinach	cabbage, celery, eggplant, strawberries	
squash	corn, nasturtiums	potatoes
strawberries	beans, borage, garlic, lettuce, onions, spinach	cabbage, cauliflower
tomatoes	asparagus, carrots, celery, chives, corn, marigolds, nasturtiums, onions, parsley	cabbage, cucumbers, fennel, kohlrabi, potatoes
turnips	peas	potatoes

Glossary

Acid soil: soil with a pH lower than 7.0

Alkaline soil: soil with a pH higher than 7.0

Annual: a plant that germinates, flowers, sets seeds and dies in one growing season

Basal leaves: leaves that form from the crown, at the base of the plant

Blanching: to deprive a plant or part of a plant of light, resulting in a pale color and usually a milder flavor

Bolting: when a plant produces flowers and seeds prematurely, usually rendering the plant inedible

Bract: a special, modified leaf at the base of a flower or inflorescence; bracts may be small or large, green or colored

Cross-pollination: the pollination of one plant by a closely related one. Undesirable if the resulting seeds or fruit lack the expected qualities; beneficial if an improved variety results

Crown: the part of the plant at or just below soil level where the shoots join the roots

Cultivar: a cultivated plant variety with one or more distinct differences from the species, e.g., in flower color or disease resistance

Damping off: fungal disease causing seedlings to rot at soil level

Deadhead: removing spent flowers to maintain a neat appearance and encourage a long blooming season

Diatomaceous earth: an abrasive dust made from the fossilized remains of diatoms, a species of algae; the scratches it makes on insect bodies causes internal fluids to leak out, and the insects die of dehydration

Direct sow: to sow seeds directly into the garden

Dormancy: a period of plant inactivity, usually during winter or unfavorable conditions

Double flower: a flower with an unusually large number of petals

Drought resistant: can withstand drought for a long time

Drought tolerant: can withstand drought conditions, but only for a limited time

Genus: a category of biological classification between the species and family levels; the first word in a scientific name indicates the genus

Half-hardy: a plant capable of surviving the climatic conditions of a given region if protected from heavy frost or cold

Harden off: to gradually acclimatize plants that have been growing in a protected environment to a harsher environment

Hardy: capable of surviving unfavorable conditions, such as cold weather or frost, without protection

Humus: decomposed or decomposing organic material in the soil

Hybrid: a plant resulting from natural or human-induced cross-breeding between varieties, species or genera

Inflorescence: an arrangement of flowers on a single stem

Invasive: able to spread aggressively and outcompete other plants

Loam: a loose soil composed of clay, sand and organic matter, often highly fertile

Microclimate: an area of beneficial or detrimental growing conditions within a larger area

Mulch: a material (e.g., shredded bark, pine cones, leaves, straw) used to surround a plant to protect it from weeds, cold or heat and to promote moisture retention

Neutral soil: soil with a pH of 7.0

Node: the area on a stem from which a leaf or new shoot grows

Perennial: a plant that takes three or more years to complete its life cycle

pH: a measure of acidity or alkalinity; soil pH influences availability of nutrients for plants

Plantlet: a young or small plant

Potager: an ornamental kitchen garden, often laid out symmetrically with raised beds or low hedge-edged beds

Rhizome: a root-like, food-storing stem that grows horizontally at or just below soil level, from which new shoots may emerge

Rosette: a low, flat cluster of leaves arranged like the petals of a rose

Runner: a modified stem that grows on the soil surface; roots and new shoots are produced at nodes along its length

Seedhead: dried, inedible fruit that contains seeds

Self-seeding: reproducing by means of seeds without human assistance, so that new plants continuously replace those that die

Single flower: a flower with a single ring of typically four or five petals

Spathe: a leaf-like bract that encloses a flower cluster or spike

Species: the fundamental unit of biological classification; the entity from which cultivars and varieties are derived

Standard: a tree or shrub pruned to form a rounded head of branches at the top of a clearly visible stem

Subspecies (subsp.): a naturally occurring, often regional, form of a species, isolated from other subspecies but still potentially interfertile with them

Taproot: a root system consisting of one long main root with smaller roots or root hairs branching from it

Tender: incapable of surviving the climatic conditions of a given region and requiring protection from frost or cold

Tuber: the thick section of a rhizome bearing nodes and buds

Understory plant: a plant that prefers to grow beneath the canopies of trees in a woodland setting

Variegation: foliage that has more than one color, often patched, striped or bearing leaf margins of a different color

Variety (var.): a naturally occurring variant of a species

Index

Boldface type refers to primary vegetable accounts.

About the Authors

Jennifer Beaver is a freelance writer and Master Gardener who discovered a passion for plants after witnessing their transformative power in neighborhoods. She helped found a group that successfully saves urban landscape trees, thereby reducing pollution and preserving property values. Captivated by the delights of vegetable gardening, she is always on the prowl for new varieties to add to her garden and her plate.

I am grateful to the many gardeners who cheerfully share their successes, failures, projects and pictures. Some I've met; others are online acquaintances. Their generosity makes me a better writer and, if not a fearless gardener, certainly a braver one.

Laura Peters is a certified, seasoned Master Gardener, garden writer and photographer with over 30 books to her credit. She has worked in almost every aspect of the horticultural industry in a career that has spanned more than 20 years. She passionately believes in organic gardening and food security, and she loves to share her knowledge with fellow gardeners and environmentalists alike.

I would like to thank my friends and family for their support and encouragement over the years. I would also like to acknowledge those who allowed us to photograph their gardens, and those who carefully grew some of the vegetables for this book. Thanks and happy gardening!